*TWAYNE'S WORLD LEADERS SERIES*

EDITOR OF THIS VOLUME

Hans Trefousse
*Brooklyn College*

*Adolphe Thiers*

TWLS 67

ADOLPHE THIERS

# ADOLPHE THIERS

*or*

## *The Triumph of the Bourgeoisie*

By RENÉ ALBRECHT-CARRIÉ

TWAYNE PUBLISHERS
A DIVISION OF G.K. HALL & CO., BOSTON

**Library of Congress Cataloging in Publication Data**


Albrecht-Carrié, René, 1904–
  Adolphe Theirs.

  (Twayne's world leaders series ; TWLS 67)
  Bibliography: p. 171–73.
  Includes index.
  1. Theirs, Adolphe, 1797–1877.   2. Statesmen—France
—Biography.
DC280.5.T5A67     944.07'092'4 [B]     77-23494
ISBN 0-8057-7717-2

to Else


The city which is composed of middle-class citizens is necessarily best governed; they are, as we say, the natural elements of a state. . . .

Thus it is manifest that the best political community is formed by citizens of the middle class. . . . Great then is the good fortune of a state in which the citizens have a moderate and sufficient property; for where some possess much, and the others nothing, there may arise an extreme democracy [in his terms a form of anarchy], or a pure oligarchy; but it is not so likely to arise out of a middle and nearly equal condition.

Benjamin Jowett's translation of Aristotle's *Politics*.

# Contents

# About the Author

René Albrecht-Carrié was born in Izmir and received his early education in the French lycée. He then came to the United States, where he attended Columbia University, from which he obtained the doctorate in history after an earlier career in mathematics. He taught at Columbia University until his retirement.

His field of interest has been diplomacy and international relations in the nineteenth and twentieth centuries, focusing particularly on western Europe. His dissertation, *Italy at the Paris Peace Conference*, was awarded the George Louis Beer prize of the American Historical Association, and his *Diplomatic History of Europe Since the Congress of Vienna* has been a standard text since its publication. Among his other works may be mentioned *Italy From Napoleon to Mussolini, France, Europe and the Two World Wars, The Meaning of the First World War, One Europe*, and *Britain and France: Adaptations to a Changing Context of Power*, a comparative analysis of foreign policies.

He has traveled extensively, particularly in western Europe, and has been the recipient of a Rockefeller grant. In 1960–61 he was a Fulbright lecturer in Italy and in 1967–68 received a Guggenheim fellowship. He has also contributed numerous articles to scholarly journals and others.

# Preface

The name of Adolphe Thiers seldom evokes today the response of familiarity; even in France his star has been somewhat in eclipse. Many other French names command better acquaintance, names likely to be associated with cultural activity. Culture, literature, and the arts may indeed justifiably be judged a more attractive, even more important and durable, aspect of man's activity than politics. Yet politics can also be seen as the resultant of the multifarious endeavors in which society indulges, so that behind its transitory aspects remains a residue of ultimate significance.

Now Thiers was above all a political animal, and his long active life coincides with the transformation that resulted in the firm implantation in France of the fundamental accomplishments of her Great Revolution. He was, as much as anyone, responsible in 1830 for the termination of Bourbon rule; and forty years later, as the chief executive of the country, he presided over the birth of the Third Republic.

What happened during that forty-year interval was the firm establishment in control of that class of society that was the mover of nineteenth-century change, the Third Estate of 1789, the bourgeoisie in later parlance. In the principles of 1789—not of 1793—Thiers was an unwavering believer, and his fight for their success is what gives consistency to his record. Those principles meant above all two things: the career open to talent, their egalitarian aspect, and rule by the qualified and the competent who could freely indulge in debate. The word *liberty* was a convenient label under which the two strands could be joined. More recently the accent has been on the egalitarian element, the integration of the mass into the body politic. Yet for all the progress of the welfare state and the curbs imposed on free enterprise, the central issue with which Thiers was concerned, the proper organization of domestic governance, in the free world at least, remains little altered.

In addition, the place and role of France in Thiers' time should be remembered. France was generally rated the most powerful state of the continent when she went through her Great Revolution. The

Napoleonic performance, though ending in defeat, seemed to confirm that estimate, even to a degree in exaggerated fashion. The events that took place between 1789 and 1815 had the effect of placing France in a position best expressed by the phrase, "when Paris catches cold Europe sneezes." It was in some respects a position comparable to that of the United States in our day.

There is another aspect to the matter. Post-Napoleonic France was not especially aggressive, but as a great power she had worldwide interests. On that score, too, Thiers had definite views. Adhering to the classical French tradition that saw in the continued fragmentation of mid Europe a condition of the country's position, Thiers observed with dismay the integrating successes (German and Italian unification) of the nationalistic force in that area. But, practical man that he was, he understood the impossibility of undoing the *fait accompli*, to which one must accommodate.

Thiers himself has often been regarded as an exponent of French nationalism. That interpretation needs qualification. He himself was no doubt responsible for bringing matters to the brink of war with England in 1840, but this result of a tactical miscalculation does not alter the fact that he was a consistent advocate of close cooperation between the two countries, which he saw in the vanguard of the progress of civilization. Nor did he ever deviate from his admiration of English political institutions which he thought France ought to take as a model.

It was the same pragmatic tendency that caused him to find uncongenial a doctrinaire approach to the form of the regime. Himself a monarchist by preference, he could accept a liberal empire, then the Republic once he became convinced that the prevalent tendency lay in that direction. More important to him was the question of the location and control of the centers of power. As he put it, "the Republic will either be conservative, or it will not be."

The present essay lays no claim to being a definitive biography of Thiers, an undertaking that its dimensions alone would preclude. It is a sketch of a political biography and an interpretation. The long and large role Thiers played in nineteenth-century France, plus the relative neglect of him in the recent period, seems ample warrant for calling attention to a figure who had definite views on the social order and a deep understanding of the political process, of which he was a highly skilled practitioner. The record of his activity remains instructive, not so much in the fallacious sense that one can learn lessons from history, as in the deeper one of contributing to the understanding of the forces that move society through the operation of politics.

# Chronology

1797  April 18. Thiers born in Marseilles.

1815  Moves to Aix to study law.

1821  Moves to Paris, joining his lifelong friend Mignet.

1821-  Journalistic activity and historical writing. Broad acquain-
1829  tance among leading personalities.

1823  First two volumes of *Histoire de la Révolution française* published.

1830  One of the founders of the newspaper *Le National*. July.
Plays a leading role in the fall of Charles X.

1832  Marries Élise Dosne, aged 16. Somewhat unorthodox ménage consists of himself, his wife, her sister, and their
mother, his father-in-law usually being elsewhere on governmental appointment.

1830-  Holds various positions in the government.
1836

1834  Received in the *Académie Française*.

1836  February-September. First prime ministership.

1840  March-October. Second prime ministership. Leads France
to the brink of war with England.

1840-  Increasingly in opposition in the Chamber.
1848

1845  First two volumes of *Histoire du Consulat et de l'Empire*.

1848  July. Revolution in Paris. Louis Philippe abdicates. The Second Republic.

1851  December. Louis Napoleon's coup d'état. Thiers arrested
and briefly in exile.

1852-  Inactive in politics. Supports Crimean War but not the war
1863  against Austria in 1859.

1862  Last volume (XX) of the *Histoire du Consulat et de l'Empire*.

1863  Return to politics. Elected to the *Corps Législatif* in Paris.
Member of the opposition.

1866-  Criticizes foreign policy of Napoleon III in the *Corps Légis-
1867  latif*.

1867  March 14. Speech in the *Corps Législatif* appraising the significance for France of the Austro-Prussian War and accu-
rately forecasting the future.

1870    Opposes the war with Prussia.

September 4. Instrumental in organization of the Provisional Government, in which he himself does not participate.

September-October. Frustrating tour of European capitals: London, Vienna, St. Petersburg, Forence.

October-November. Negotiates armistice and surrender of Paris with Bismarck.

1871    February 8. Election of National Assembly. Thiers elected in 26 *départements*, chooses Paris.

February 17. Designated "Chief of the executive power of the French Republic." Is simultaneously chief executive, prime minister, and ordinary member of the Assembly.

February. Negotiates terms of peace with Bismarck.

March 1. Terms of peace accepted by the Assembly.

March-May. Parisian Commune. Plays leading role in the recapture of Paris by French troops and the crushing of the Commune.

August 30. His title changed to "President of the Republic."

1871-  In conflict with the Royalist majority of the National Assem-
1873    bly. Plays important role in task of reconstruction, the raising of loans for payment of the war indemnity, and the departure of German troops.

1873    May 24. Resigns the presidency, succeeded by Marshal MacMahon. Continues as ordinary deputy in the Assembly.

1875    January 30. By a one-vote majority the Wallon amendment is accepted, formally making "Republic" the name of the regime.

1877    May 16. MacMahon's "coup d'état," an attempt to assert the right of the executive to dismiss ministers. Thiers among those voting no confidence in the government.

Candidate for the election scheduled for October.

September 3. Dies suddenly from a stroke.

# CHAPTER 1

# The Formative Years, 1797–1821

A DOLPHE Thiers was born in Marseilles on April 18, 1797. That
was the time when, the excessive ardor of the revolutionary
urge having spent itself, a transitional period of uncertain direction
was paving the way for the imposition of the Napoleonic order.
When that régime came to its Waterloo, Thiers was eighteen years
of age, a young man ready to launch upon whatever career would fill
the rest of his existence.

His initial conditioning, his education, therefore took place during the imperial régime, the shape and the impact of which must be
remembered in any account of his later activity, bearing in mind the
validity of the platitude that the child is father to the man. Napoleon
had mainly done two things for France. He had made good beyond
retrieval the break with the *ancien régime,* in which respect his
claim that he was a son of the Revolution may be granted; he had
also provided her with glory, mainly of the military kind to be sure,
but as a consequence with a sense of confident power. The defeated
France of 1815, in contrast with the victorious one of a century later,
was not obsessed by the negative fear of insecurity.

When Napoleon lost the sense of the possible and embarked upon
the eventually fatal adventures that led him into Spain and into
Russia, the French people began to grow weary of the too strenuous
price of glory and there was relief at his first departure in 1814. But
one can only be surprised at the brief time that that emotion lasted.
Louis XVIII, brought back in the baggage of the victorious allies,
was received with but scant enthusiasm, and for the overwhelming
mass of the French people the white flag of the Bourbons evoked
memories that commanded very dubious popularity. Less than a
year after his relegation to Elban exile Napoleon found wide response in France and experienced little difficulty in raising a new
army. The reason for this must be seen in the two contributions that

15

have just been indicated, plus the fact that a whole new generation had grown up since the Revolution, wholly innocent of the ways of pre-1789 France. Thiers himself was a member of it.

Thiers was too young to have experienced military service. He had therefore grown up in peace and gone to school in the newly organized system of Napoleonic education. His very modest background did not give him automatic entrée to the Establishment of the day. His father was of little use to him, whatever influence he may have had being mainly the negative one of the memory of abandonment.[1] The child was as a consequence left to the exclusive care of his mother and his maternal grandmother, both of them ardent Royalists.

The young Adolphe may have inherited the quick wit of his father, but as a child showed none of the paternal irregular tendencies. He was a good student in school, obtaining a scholarship that enabled him to attend the lycée. The mark he made in that establishment, in both literary and scientific disciplines, his sharp mind, and his articulateness, caused him to accept the advice to enroll in the university of neighboring Aix where he went at the end of 1815, accompanied by his mother and grandmother, with a view to studying law. What better introduction to the possibility of making his way for a young man devoid of connections or resources?

Though only fifteen miles away, Aix was, as it still is, very different from Marseilles. A mere fraction of the latter in dimensions, Aix's broad avenues lined with trees and patrician houses bespeak repose and dignity in marked contrast with the bustling activity of the great seaport where the whole Mediterranean meets, truly a melting pot since the time of its Greek origins. The prevailing climate in Aix was conducive to intellectual application, and there also Thiers made his mark as a quick and avid learner, an assiduous student, though not averse to an occasional prank and to convivial student gatherings. Whether or not his verbal articulateness is to be credited to his mother's partly Greek descent, the fact is that he was a facile and fluent talker, as he continued to be throughout his life. Also at Aix he met François Mignet, a common interest in history helping to create a bond between the two, and their friendship remained unclouded so long as they both lived.

Despite the Royalist leanings of his maternal tutors Thiers was already acquiring a reputation for liberal tendencies, and an episode may be cited as an indication of this fact as well as of his facile industry. Shortly after his graduation the University of Aix offered a prize for an essay the subject of which was to be an *Éloge de Vauvenargues.*[2] Thiers entered the competition, but the quality of his contribution, the authorship of which was suspected although it was submitted under seal, in combination with his liberal reputation, resulted in the compromise solution of postponement of the award. Warned by a friendly member of the awarding jury, Thiers, undaunted, resorted to a subterfuge. With the utmost expeditiousness he proceeded to write a different version of the *Éloge,* one more acceptable to a conservative jury, and had it sent to Aix under a Paris postmark. His calculation proved correct for the essay received the first prize, but one may judge the consternation of the jury when, upon identifying the authors, they discovered that the first and the second prizes had gone to the same man.

A brief quotation tells us as much about the author as about the subject of the essay:

The world, according to Vauvenargues, is what it must be, that is to say rife with obstacles; for, in order for action to take place, there must be difficulties to overcome, and evil is thus accounted for. Life itself is an act, and whatever the cost of it, the exertion of our energy is sufficient to give us satisfaction, because it is the fulfilment of the laws of our being. Such in essence is the doctrine of Vauvenargues. He is considered an amiable genius, a consoling philosopher; one thing alone need be said: he had understood the universe, and the universe well understood is not discouraging, but rather offers sublime possibilities.[3]

And the lapse of almost a decade only confirmed his appraisal of the essential nature and purpose of human activity. Writing in the *Revue française* in November 1829 on the memoirs of Gouvion Saint-Cyr,[4] Thiers had the following to say:

Those who have dreamt of perpetual peace knew neither the nature of man nor his fate in this world. The universe is a vast field of action, and man is born to act. Whether or not he be fated to happiness, it is certain in any case that life is only bearable for him when he acts with determination; it is only then that he forgets himself, is carried away, and ceases using his mind to doubt, curse, become corrupt and do evil.

The unique place of Paris in France is sufficiently known. The Revolution and Napoleon, whatever else they may have done, had

in this respect the effect of continuity where it came to the centraliz-
ing trend, the country's organization, to which they both made a
further contribution. Paris almost inevitably sucked to itself any
young Frenchman of ambition, and thither Thiers went. He rejoined his faithful friend Mignet, who had preceded him to the
capital, in the very modest lodgings that were all that their limited
circumstances could provide. It is no exaggeration to say that, in the
following years, Thiers set about the conquest of Paris, which meant
in turn the achievement of a high position in France.

We must pause here for a moment to consider the condition of the
country at the time Thiers arrived in the capital. The six years since
the second return of Louis XVIII may best be looked upon under
two heads, the domestic and the international, a distinction especially relevant in view of Thiers' subsequent career.

France of the Restoration seemed to embark at first upon a course
of sensible compromise and moderation. Brother of the unfortunate
Louis XVI, the new king, sixty years of age upon his accession, was
himself no outstanding man. But he understood that certain changes
could not be undone, and, as he put it, he had had enough of travel
and wanted above all to end his days in peace on the French throne.
He therefore, out of his love for his people, and, interestingly, upon
Tsar Alexander's advice, granted them a charter. To be sure, article
14 of the document implied the right of withdrawal, since freely
granted, but in effect, albeit at the king's gracious pleasure and on
the basis of an extremely limited franchise, the French people were
to enjoy the boon of representative institutions not substantially
different from those that prevailed across the Channel.

Some of the returning émigrés were less sensible than the king;
they were bent on revenge and the passage of the White Terror[5]
followed. The very limited franchise had the effect of returning a
Chamber more Royalist than the king himself. The 1815 *Chambre
introuvable* was shortly dismissed, to be followed in September by a
more moderate body, and for a few years the path of mild liberalism
was pursued under ministries led first by Richelieu, then Desolles
and Decazes. In 1819 a more liberal press law was promulgated.

But the following year an incident resulted in the adoption of an
altered course. The Duc de Berry, presumptive heir to the crown in
the absence of issue from the king and his remaining brother, was
assassinated. Although the act was that of an individual fanatic, it
served to induce the government to adopt a policy of repression. A

more restrictive electoral law in 1820 further reduced the roll of an already minuscule electorate and produced the expected in the form of the new parliamentary majority, a trend that was to continue for the rest of the decade of the 1820s.

At the level of states, revolutionary and Napoleonic France had been the source of such disturbance that even the return of the Bourbons did not totally allay the fears of others, whether on the score of the revolutionary ideology or on the simple one of power. It should not be forgotten that the France of almost two centuries ago was the most populous state of Europe—until the turn of the century the French population exceeded even the Russian—and the most advanced one on the continent. And one may recall the decree of the National Convention on November 19, 1792, just when the tide of war had turned and the armies of the Revolution were carrying the war and the revolutionary idea into enemy lands where they were not always initially unwelcome: "The National Convention declares that it will grant assistance and fraternity to all peoples who wish to recover their liberty."[6] It had not been an empty threat.

The egalitarian idea had struck deep roots that even the opposition to it in France herself made it impossible to eradicate. That aspect of the situation could be acceptable to the constitutional monarchy that was Britain, but even Tsar Alexander did not long adhere to his liberal velleities. However, as the years passed, France of the Restoration as a state among states seemed to behave; in 1818 her war indemnity was finally discharged and at Aix-la-Chapelle she received a certificate of good behavior in the form of full reintegration into the European Concert. But it must also be remembered that the settlement of 1815, mild and reasonable as it may seem by the standards of more recent practice, was widely resented in France where it was often referred to as the "iniquitous" peace.

By the time Napoleon died at St. Helena in 1821 the Napoleonic legend had achieved considerable prosperity, and if the charge of aggressive intent would be unwarranted, the consciousness of a primacy that tended to be taken for granted ran deep among the French. It was not a totally empty boast; the status of Paris as the capital of European culture was widely recognized abroad. Things have changed since the beginning of the nineteenth century, though the French are still often believed to be devotees of *la gloire*.

CHAPTER 2

# Thiers and the Restoration

## I *Journalistic Beginnings*

SUCH was the France in which, in September 1821, Thiers made his entrance upon the Parisian stage. He hardly made an impressive appearance, a somewhat uncouth and diminutive youth—he was little over 5 feet tall—with a marked marseillais accent, this last a source of condescending attraction among the socially polished. But of these handicaps, if handicaps they were, Thiers seems to have been totally unaware; at any rate they induced no reticence or timidity on his part. Of his capacities he was fully conscious and faced people and situations with seemingly complete confidence.

What Thiers would do was not predetermined, save that the word, spoken or written, was obviously the most valuable asset in his armory, an asset that, to repeat, he used with great facility and virtually no reticence. In a gathering he was apt to take over, yet not offensively to others, for he usually had intelligent and relevant observations to make. A recommendation he carried from Aix led to a first opening, at the *Constitutionnel*, where he soon joined the editorial board, while he also contributed to the *Globe*, both papers that may be classified as critics of the regime. Thiers seemed headed for a journalistic career.

The range of his competence was apparently unlimited, meaning that he would with assurance write on any subject. This might be expected to imply superficiality, but that would be the wrong word; not profundity to be sure, but facility would be nearer the mark. Sainte-Beuve may be quoted on Thiers' accounts in the *Constitutionnel* of the salon of 1822, accounts that reveal at the very least a keen eye and an open mind; he certainly was in the vanguard of those that gave the new tendencies in art recognition.

Whatever, [wrote Sainte-Beuve] he himself may think of them today the author [of these articles], very critical of his early essays and since grown mature in these matters, I can assure him that one can still read the collection of them with pleasure and profit. If the historical survey of the revolution in painting is infinitely deficient and can hardly be taken into account where Italy, that Thiers had not yet visited, is concerned, the broad considerations on taste, on art criticism and on the peculiar merits of drawing remain pages that are very pleasing and sound, pages that reveal a very sure instinct and a naturally enlightened judgement. The considerations on Gérard's *Corinne au Cap Misène* lead to an appreciation of Madame de Stael's portrait that may be found severe but are nevertheless full of good sense. . . . This same *Salon of 1822* contains generous advice to Horace Vernet and a commemorative page for the young Drouais, David's first pupil. . . .[1]

The key to Thiers' unquestionably remarkable performance lay in two things: an enormous capacity for work and for the absorption and the retention of information which he would then retail with assurance.

Thiers' day began at five o'clock in the morning and thereafter was full of activity. When his economic circumstances had improved, which was quite early, he took great pride in a horse he had acquired and that he used for exercise. But his editorial work did not suffice to fill his time, and as his circle of acquaintances widened and he became an increasingly known figure in the capital, his evenings would often be spent in salons where he frequently would become the center of a group to which he would expatiate on all manner of topics, from politics through military campaigns of the past to the theater and the arts. Thiers seemed to be one of those people who could thrive on minimal sleep.

During the year 1820 outbreaks of liberal agitation had occurred in various parts of Europe, the Italian and the Germanic states among them. Over that whole domain Metternich presided, an intelligent man and a skillful manipulator who genuinely believed in the merits of the old order. He stood against the trend of history, yet for the better part of half a century he successfully managed to stem the tide of change in mid Europe. As much as anyone Metternich was the organizer and director of the system that, in 1815, had created the international of rulers, essentially a coalition of the three conservative states of Europe, Austria, Prussia, and Russia, dedi-

cated to the preservation of the *ancien régime* type of order, at the
domestic no less than at the international level.

This implied as a corollary the legitimacy of intervention in the
domestic affairs of a state, should a success of the revolutionary idea
anywhere threaten to become a center of possibly contagious infection. Here was one important aspect of the Concert of Europe, the
other being the preservation of the international equilibrium. Metternich had learned the lesson of the Great Revolution in France.

He had his way in Italy, when the Congresses of Troppau and
Laibach, at the turn from 1820 to 1821, sanctioned Austrian intervention in Naples. The Austrians experienced little difficulty in restoring King Ferdinand to his proper autocratic position in Naples,
where the grant of a constitution had been extracted from him the
preceding July. On their way the Austrians performed a similar
service for the King of Sardinia and for the Pope who had also been
faced with insurrections. All Italy in her various divisions was
brought back under proper governance, the operation incidentally
confirming the paramountcy of Austrian control in the peninsula.

This last aspect of things was less attractive to French power, but
the turn to reaction in that country in the year 1820 has been mentioned. In the domain of internal arrangements reactionary Restoration France and Metternich largely agreed. But there was another
focus of revolutionary infection; in 1820 also, King Ferdinand of
Spain had been compelled to restore an earlier constitution, the
liberal one of 1812. The Spanish case was similar to the Neapolitan
in its larger implications, and it was equally appropriate that Europe
should take cognizance of it.

This was the chief purpose of the Congress of Verona in October
1822. But just as Austria was the logical candidate for carrying out
the European mandate of intervention in Italy, the facts of geography pointed to France as the logical candidate for a similar operation in Spain—the Tsar's offer to send a Russian army across Europe
to Spain was looked askance at by all. But at this point certain
difficulties arose at the international as well as the domestic level.
The British did not feel particularly exercised at the grant of constitutions. In the Italian case their condoning of the Austrian intervention was based rather on considerations of power, their willingness to regard Italy as part of the Austrian sphere of influence. But
French intervention in Spain seemed to them an altogether differ-

ent matter and the British foreign secretary, Canning, had opposed the decisions of Verona. As to the government of Louis XVIII, it was of two minds about Spain, uncertain for one thing about using an army in which the Napoleonic tradition was still alive in the ranks, not to mention the strength of the liberal tendency in the country. Also, what would be the Spanish reaction to the reappearance of French troops a mere ten years after their eviction from the country?

In the end, a French army went into Spain where it, too, had little difficulty in restoring the king to his autocratic position, while the operation resulted in some minor military prestige for France. Thiers' role in the episode was essentially confined to that of a journalist. He wanted to see for himself and betook himself to the Pyrenees, though not without some difficulty, for he already was an object of surveillance. He took a circuitous route, travelling first to unrelated Geneva, thence by way of Aix and Marseilles, where he renewed acquaintances, to the Spanish border. The reports of his activity that were sent back by the local *préfets* indicated nothing subversive, and the outcome of his brief expedition, barely touching Spain, was a reportage eventually collected in a book, *Les Pyrénées et le Midi de la France pendant les mois de novembre et décembre 1823.*

Considering Thiers' already established and well-known liberal leanings, his position on the score of the French intervention in Spain may seem surprising, for he was in favor of it. His argument was based on what he regarded as the affinity between the interests of the two countries, of which the dynastic connection was expression, and he feared that a liberal regime in Spain might adopt an anti-French stance. This position of his is especially worth mentioning for it shows at a very early stage a tendency to which he would consistently adhere throughout his political career. If he held strong views on matters social and political, Theirs was also above all practical, a practitioner of *Realpolitik* and a consistent defender of the national interest; he would not be deflected by (to him) irrelevant ideological considerations. The operation of this factor will be seen on later occasions when he himself was in a position of governmental power or spoke out in parliament as a critic of the policies of a particular administration.[2] In 1823 the government of Louis XVIII had no reason to fear that Thiers would engage in subversive activity on the Spanish border.

## II  *Beginnings of Thiers as Historian*

Thiers' journalistic work and the social activity that increasingly went with it did not suffice to absorb his overabundant energy. Like his friend Mignet, history interested him, especially the immediate background of his own time, the great event of the Revolution and its Napoleonic sequel under which his own youth had unfolded. Early in 1822 he contracted for the publication of a history of the Revolution; his age and the fact that he was still little known caused the publishers to insist on the association of an older established writer, Félix Bodin. Thiers set to work with his accustomed vigor and the following year the first two volumes of the *Histoire de la Révolution Française* appeared, presumably the work of joint authorship. But thereafter Bodin withdrew from the collaboration and Thiers completed the work alone, adding another eight volumes to the first two, all in a period of four years.[3]

The book was an enormous success, 200,000 copies of it being sold in a short time. It is one of the earliest works on the subject, a fact that makes it at once important and superseded. The initial part especially was done in haste, the reason why it was recast, but greater care went into the subsequent volumes. The reasons for its being superseded, apart from a degree of carelessness in verifying data, are the limitation of the sources available as well as that of the treatment.

The work is, in the main, political history of the narrative kind, though appreciable notice is taken of economic and financial factors, and we have since (or at least think we have), admittedly with mixed success, delved deeper under the surface of events. But the narrative is vivid and effective, adequately conveying the sense of high purpose as well as of appalling confusion, especially at such times as the critical days when the Revolution was threatened by combined internal opposition and almost universal war to the accompaniment of chaotic financial conditions, or at the climax of the Robespierrean terror. To give an illustration in Thiers' own words:

On the first commemoration of the 14th of July, in 1790, the revolution was still innocent and kindly disposed, and as a consequence might not have been serious and even been put an end to by foreign bayonets; but in August 1793 it had taken on the aura of tragedy, marked by victories and defeats, and had become serious as a revolution that was both irrevocable and heroic.[4]

Or again:

> There is a truth that must always be repeated, namely that passion is
> never wise or enlightened, but that passion alone is capable of saving
> peoples under conditions of extreme stress.[5]

Thiers was especially interested and had competence in certain
particular matters. Finance, not least his own as we shall see, he
understood, and to military matters he devoted considerable attention. He made a point of acquainting himself with maps and with
ordnance, discussing campaigns with military men, whom he often
impressed by his quick grasp of situations, and could even use to
good purpose direct exchanges with the great Jomini.[6] His accounts
of the 1792 campaign, the turning point of Valmy, and of the Italian
campaigns of Napoleon make stirring reading to this day.

The book began to appear in 1823, a quarter of a century after the
end of the revolutionary upheaval proper, when the transition that
was the Directory was about to give way to Napoleon. A generation
had grown up since that time, but many who had had personal
experience of the events of the hectic decade were still living, so
that Thiers could avail himself of the first-hand recollections of wit-
nesses, a source he exploited with persistent assiduity. Sufficient
time had passed for quieter appraisal, yet not so much as to make
the period dead past. To the French of the Restoration the record of
the twenty-five years of turmoil that preceded the reestablishment
of the old order was full of fascination, and in this lies one important
reason for the popularity of the work.

Also, being among the first in the field, Thiers' *History of the
French Revolution* had considerable influence in shaping subsequent views. That is the reason why, though his rating as an
historian is not especially high,[7] he nevertheless holds an important
place among the craft, his work offering a coherent view and interpretation. Thiers was never an academic; a political man of action
above all, ever involved in the live issues of the day, his history is as
much a political tract as a work of literary scholarship. The *History*
thus provides an invaluable clue to his own way of thinking and an
important key to his entire future career.

The following passage is worth noting:

> Since the days when Tacitus saw it applaud the crimes of the emperors,
> the vile mob has never changed. Always sudden in its movements, one day

it erects altars to the country *(patrie)*, the next raises scaffolds, and is only beautiful and noble to observe when, trained in the army, it rushes against the enemy battalions. Let not despotism blame the crimes of the mob on liberty; for under despotism it was as guilty as under the republic. We always advocate enlightenment and education for those barbarians, teeming at the bottom of the social scale and ever ready to besmirch society with all their crimes, responsive to the appeal of any power, and dishonoring all causes.[8]

Yet in the large sense Thiers approved of the Revolution, the main contribution of which, in his view, was the abolition of privilege, the egalitarian opening of opportunities, the career open to talent, a condition of which he himself was an example and a beneficiary. In 1789 and throughout the nineteenth century, in France and many other places, this meant the bourgeoisie coming into its own, a class of which Thiers himself was the perfect personification.

Thiers was a monarchist, and the constitution of 1791 earned his approval. But for a time thereafter the Revolution had gone off the rails and indulged in excesses for which he expressed unqualified condemnation. The September massacres, the role of the mob, he depicted in their full horror, and doctrinaire Robespierre, quoted at length throughout the *History,* emerges without redeeming features, the very antithesis of Thiers' own practical reasonableness. Yet, on balance and overall, he could accept, if not condone, the role of violence in achieving the larger purpose.[9] Thus, during the Restoration, Thiers belonged in the category of liberal politics. The restored monarchy with the Charter, constitutionalism on the English model, represented for him the best ordering of the state. We shall presently observe the influence of this outlook in 1830.

Since we have been speaking of Thiers as a literary man, his views in matters of style are of interest. Bearing in mind Buffon's dictum that *le style c'est l'homme,* the following passage from the *National* is significant:

We can no longer have the grandeur, at once sublime and naive, that belonged to Bossuet and Pascal, and which characterized their century as well; we cannot even any longer display the finesse, the grace, the exquisite naturalness of Voltaire. That time is past; but a style that is simple, truthful, deliberate, a style that is scientifically wrought is what is possible for us to produce. It is not a bad fate when one uses it to tell important truths. The style of Laplace's *Exposition du système du monde*, of Napoleon's memoirs, those are models of the simple thought and language suited to our age.[10]

And this judgment by Chateaubriand may also be cited:

M. Thiers combines low habits with an elevated instinct. I see in him a mind that is supple, quick, subtle and flexible, perhaps the heir of the future, capable of understanding everything save the grandeur of moral order; devoid of envy, pettiness and prejudice, he stands out against the background of the mediocrities of our time. . . . M. Thiers may become a great minister or remain a meddler,[11]. . .

as well as a very early and prescient appraisal based on some writings in a report to the Duke of La Rochefoucauld-Liancourt, who considered employing him in a secretarial capacity:

I have studied and appraised the new pamphlet and my judgement is the same as yours. In two or three chapters one can discern signs of statesmanship, in many others sophistry, and rhetoric everywhere. A few pages are written in good style, but it is most uneven in most of the rest. . . . Sermonizing and pathos are mixed together, and this is very regrettable, for there are indeed, expressed with brilliancy and in considerable number, most novel and excellent insights.[12]

Thiers, obviously, was not without his critics, but space does not allow more extensive quotations.

### III  *The Reign of Charles X*

By 1823, if Thiers approved of the intervention in Spain, the reactionary course of governmental direction he could only find increasingly distasteful. In 1824 Louis XVIII died, having achieved his wish of not having to indulge in further travel. The crown passed to the last of the three brothers, as Charles X, the embodiment of the *ancien régime* at its most intransigeant. A limited and bigoted man, the charge against the Bourbons that they were equally incapable of learning or forgetting fitted him to perfection.

More important, however, was the specific legislation that irked the bourgeois class, potentially the most dependable bulwark of the regime. The law of indemnity in 1825, designed to compensate losses incurred by victims of the Revolution, mainly émigré aristocrats, was all the more resented that it was in part at the expense of holders of government bonds, the rate of whose return was diminished.

Without a doubt the overwhelming majority of the French people were Catholic, as the Napoleonic Concordat had acknowledged. But among the educated class iconoclastic and often anticlerical Voltairianism had made deep and lasting inroads. That influence persisted despite some religious revival, reaction to the excesses of the Revolution. But instead of leaving well enough alone, here again Charles X went too far. The law of sacrilege in 1826, making certain "sacrilegious" offenses punishable by law, was regarded by many as an obscurantist irritant, extreme expression of an attempt to give the Church a position of favor. The disbanding of the National Guard the following year worked to the same effect of antagonizing the bourgeois class, proud of that institution that it regarded as peculiarly its own.

Over these retrograde enactments the ultra-conservative Villèle appropriately presided as the king's first minister, while Charles X himself seemed unaware of the rising discontent. His confidence was sufficiently mistaken for him to call an election at the end of 1827. Restricted as the franchise was, the result nonetheless was a liberal success, indication of the depth and extent of the opposition to what many regarded as antediluvian policies. For the moment the king yielded, replacing Villèle by the more moderate Martignac, but Martignac proved to be too conservative for the liberals and too liberal for the Ultras.

He was dismissed in August 1829, his position given to the Prince de Polignac, a man definitely not of the nineteenth century. His private wire to the divinity in the form of visions of the Virgin Mary, authentic as these may have been to him, was hardly a suitable approach to the politics of the day, and the fantastic scheme that he proposed for a far-reaching rearrangement of Europe likewise bears witness to the nature of his contact with reality.[13] The fact that the king retained Polignac in office despite his failure of support in the Chamber raised the constitutional issue of the locus and division of power. Charles X was embarking upon a crucial test and upon the last year of his reign. But before dealing with the events of the year 1830 we must briefly pause to consider the progress of Thiers during the second half of the 1820s.

We left him engaged in journalistic work, bringing out the first volumes of his *History of the French Revolution*, and, despite his endorsement of the Spanish intervention, already known as definitely in the liberal camp, meaning the opposition to the rule of Charles X. His activity during these years may be summed up as laying the bases for a role of leadership in the future. This he did through his continued journalistic activity as well as through a steady enlargement of his circle of connections.

His writings brought him to the attention of Talleyrand. Entering the eighth decade of his life, Talleyrand's ability to survive, while usually serving in important capacities all the regimes from the *ancien* to the Restoration, had endowed him with an aura of seeming indestructibility. Though he had been instrumental in contriving the smooth return of Louis XVIII and had served him and France well at the Congress of Vienna, Talleyrand was currently not involved in the government; his wide experience of affairs, French in particular, caused him to smell approaching trouble. Highly intelligent and truly civilized, equally cynical and unprincipled, unless a keen sense and acceptance of the possible, a pragmatic approach, be called principle, he was highly respected in the role of elder statesman. The honors and wealth he had accumulated through his services and his peculations he thoroughly enjoyed, whether in his Parisian residence or his gracious country retreat of Valençay.

Thiers was anxious to make Talleyrand's acquaintance, well aware of the latter's merit and influence. When the two finally met, Talleyrand was somewhat surprised to find Thiers favoring the Spanish expedition, recalling that he himself had seen in Spain the beginning of the downfall of Napoleon. Keen judge of men that he was, Talleyrand, however, thought he detected in the rising young scribbler the makings of an outstanding career. Thiers thus gained entrée both to a distinguished circle of important people and to a valuable source of advice in the person of the Prince of Benevento, who in addition gave him the benefit of a firsthand account of many of the things Thiers was busy writing about; Talleyrand was a first-class living source for his *History*. Besides all this Thiers also made a favorable impression on the Duchess of Dino, Talleyrand's niece and companion. She, too, proved to be a keen and useful source of information, though rather about contemporary affairs than past history; between the two an intimate correspondence developed that lasted many years, and it has even been suggested that the relationship between them exceeded the bounds of the purely platonic.

Thiers had gained full access into the Establishment, both literary and political, and on it he was making a decided impression. Totally unselfconscious and undeterred by the impression that his stature and accent would make at first meeting, he would volubly expatiate on almost any subject. As already indicated, facile he may have been rather than profound, but what he had to say was relevant and the range of his competence was impressive.

The rapidity of Thiers' rise is remarkable and it is not surprising that it should have matched that of his personal fortune. No financial irregularities are implied but connections are always useful, and it must be remembered that the standards of probity of the day were looser than those that have supposedly come to prevail in our time. What might now be regarded as a financial irregularity, and call for an investigation by the courts or a public body, was then often taken for granted.

For that matter there was nothing of special favor or connection in the appreciable income that was produced by his writing. He had come penniless to Paris in 1821, yet by the end of the decade his *History of the French Revolution* alone had brought a handsome return of some 57,000 francs,[14] a sum worth rather more in terms of purchasing power than the same amount in present-day dollars. His partnership in the directorship of the *Constitutionnel*, while certainly the result of merit, although in that case connections helped, was also a valuable asset.

### CHAPTER 3

# 1830—Thiers as Kingmaker

### I  *Preliminaries: The Breakdown of a System*

AS the decade was drawing to a close the pressure of dissatisfaction with the government was building up to a climax. We have seen the expression of Charles X's insensitivity to the surrounding conditions in his recalling Polignac to head the ministry in 1829. It took just under a year before the explosion took place, an upheaval in which Thiers was to play a major role.[1]

Two seemingly unrelated events at the opening of the year 1830 may be mentioned as symbolic of the Parisian climate of the day. On January 3, a new publication, *Le National*, made its appearance. It was founded by Thiers in collaboration with his friend Mignet and the more radically inclined Armand Carrel.[2] Thiers was responsible for having arranged the financing of the paper and was to have the main direction of it during the first year of its existence.

On February 25 the Comédie Française put on for the first time Victor Hugo's drama *Hernani*. The occasion turned into a riot, though for literary rather than political reasons. The play was in a sense a manifesto of the Romantic movement reaching its heyday in France at this time, and was cheered by the adherents of that movement with the same vigor that went into the attack from classicist ranks. But it is also worth noting that the hero, Hernani, was a rebel.

In matters literary Hugo and Thiers represented contrast, Thiers personifying the solid bourgeois virtues. And it was correspondingly appropriate that the two men should hold equally disparaging opinions of each other. Though Thiers himself attended the performance, having addressed himself directly to Hugo to obtain a loge, and the *National* gave the play a guarded but on the whole favorable notice, Thiers' view of Hugo is best expressed in his later (in 1849) comment: "That little fool of Victor Hugo." Hugo's opinion of Thiers was the following: "I have always had for this famous statesman, this eminent orator, this mediocre writer, this small and narrow heart, an indefinable feeling made up of combined admiration, aversion and contempt."[3] Nevertheless, romantic hope and solid bourgeois stodginess were both components of the 1830 revolution, and it is precisely the conjunction of the two that resulted in its ambiguous and frustrating outcome.

Though the *National* started out on a tone of moderately ambivalent criticism of the regime it was not long before it ran afoul of the censorship. But the fact that the subscription that was opened to meet the payment of the one-thousand-franc fine that was imposed by the courts was largely oversubscribed took on the color of a plebiscite of sorts—a Gallup poll would be our current test—and was an indication of the direction in which the wind was blowing. Thanking the subscribers in somewhat grandiloquent language, Thiers wrote: "If we do not wish to cross the Channel, we may cross the Atlantic."

Monarchist Thiers, as mentioned before, approved of the 1791 constitution and bemoaned the excesses of the Revolution, even if on balance he found them understandable. In totally transparent language, he was reminding Charles X of what had happened forty years before to the French ruler of the day. If the moderate English example of the Glorious Revolution that had established constitutional rule in that country was not followed in France, the American republican model might be adopted. Looking over Thiers' career and the course of nineteenth-century French events, the warning may seem prescient rather than pompous. But we must not anticipate our story and for the moment must adhere to the events of 1830.

The reply of the reconvened Chamber in March to the address from the throne voiced criticism rather than acquiescence. Thereupon the king had recourse to dissolution, but another election in May merely confirmed his misjudgment. There began to be talk of the possibility of a coup d'état on the part of the king who might assume full powers under the emergency provisions of the Charter, while in effect denying the spirit of that document. Wherein lay the emergency save in the king's refusal to adhere to his constitutional role?

At this point a digression, or an attempt at one, occurred. The North African coast, the Maghreb, entertained commercial relations with Europe, but its harbors were also the havens of piratical activity; the American marines in Tripoli and the English punitive expedition to Algiers in 1816 may be recalled. Certain involved transactions, which it would take too long to retail,[4] led to a dispute involving France, and the insult of the French consul by the Bey of Algiers was the pretext for avenging French honor. This is the just-mentioned digression which took the form of a French naval demonstration that resulted in the capture of Algiers on July 5, the beginning of the long tale of French involvement in North Africa. The news of the event reached Paris on the 9th. Thiers was opposed to the adventure, of which it will suffice to say at this point that it failed of its diversionary intent where French domestic affairs were concerned.

## II   Les Trois Glorieuses

Foolishly blind and self-confident, the king resorted to the coup d'état. That is at least a not unfair description of the famous five ordinances that appeared in the *Moniteur* on July 26, opening the passage to those days that have gone down in French annals, those of the Left at least, as *les trois glorieuses,* the three-day 1830 revolution in France. The Chamber was again dissolved and the suffrage still further restricted with a view to insuring an amenable conservative majority; the freedom of the press was also further curtailed. This action, definitely extralegal, was justified on the plea of the higher necessity of maintaining orderly government, a condition of which the king claimed the right to be judge.

But it is an interesting measure of the degree of his misjudgment that no precautions were taken for the preservation of order in the capital, the necessity of which it needed no unusual perspicacity to expect. The military force available was small, and Marmont, to whom the command of it was to be given should the necessity arise, was not even informed, while the king left St. Cloud to hunt in Rambouillet. The report of the English ambassador seems adequate summation of the prevalent climate in governmental circles: "When I go to the foreign office I have the impression of entering Milton's paradise of fools."[5]

The opposition press reacted with indignation. Meeting in the offices of the *National,* its representatives entrusted Thiers with the drafting of a collective protest, which they all—forty-three of them—proceeded to sign. Among other things the manifesto stated that

The rule of legality is broken; that of force has begun. . . . Obedience is no longer a duty. . . . We shall try to publish our newspapers without asking for the required authorization. . . . It is not for us to tell the dissolved Chamber where its duty lies; but we can beg it, in the name of France, to use its evident right, and to resist, as much as it will find it possible, the violation of the laws. . . .[6]

and went on to conclude:

The government has lost the attribute of legality on which obedience depends. As far as we are concerned we oppose it; it is for France to judge how far our opposition should go.[7]

The manifesto was published in the *National* and the *Temps* and widely broadcast throughout the city, then the country. Though the intention may not have been that of an appeal to popular insurrection, the protest could easily be interpreted as such.

Given the available means of communication of the time, it would take some days for the country to become aware of events at the center of government. But here the crucial role of Paris in centralized France, especially in revolutionary France, must be emphasized. A city of some 600,000, far larger than any other in the country, Paris had the resource of a large proletariat, and the memory of Parisian *journées* at the height of the Great Revolution was not dead.

But here another factor intruded, the distinction between the mass—or the mob—and the revolutionary leadership, a distinction that was to give the 1830 revolution its character and decide its peculiar outcome. Anticipating the subsequent course of events, it may be said that the leadership used the mass to insure its own success, but that the difference between the two elements was considerable, with the consequence that the episode had the effect of perpetuating the cleavage of the country in two, a division that was to give instability to its governmental arrangements and to lead to change through violence and numerous attempts at constitution drafting. Here lies the central characteristic of the political life of France ever since her first Great Revolution, the unreconciled social division of the country.

The epithet *liberal* could serve as a momentary basis of agreement in the defense of liberty against the abuses of arbitrary power. But the leadership was overwhelmingly bourgeois. Thiers himself, who stands out as much as anyone among that leadership, was a staunch believer in property and order, as well as a convinced believer in the prerogatives of his own, the bourgeois, class.

For the liberalism of the day the issue was still the same as in 1789, opposition to arbitrary, absolute power. Hence the great emphasis on constitution, the red flag of the time. In the pages of the *Constitutionnel* Thiers had expatiated on the merits of the English example. As he put it on many occasions, he was a defender of legality and it was only the breach of that legality by the government that justified opposition, even violent opposition if no other course was available, in defense of that legality. The abuse was what had brought about the downfall of Charles I of England as well as that of Napoleon.

In any case the atmosphere was tense in Paris at the close of the day on July 26, and the cry "Long live the Charter! Down with the ministers!" could be heard in street gatherings. The next morning the police seized the liberal papers and impounded their presses, while various elements, republicans, students, members of such secret societies as *Aide-toi, le ciel t'aidera*, began to coalesce and barricades were erected in the populous eastern quarter of the city.

The belated and inadequate use of armed force on the 28th led to violent encounters which on the whole turned in favor of the insurrection, the leadership of which had by now passed into republican—meaning the more radical tendency—hands. The tricolor flag of the Republic flew over the Hôtel de Ville, and the army, some elements of which had joined the insurgents, was pulled out of the city. By this time Charles X's willingness to withdraw the ordinances and recast the ministry was too late and had become irrelevant. So was his attempt to transfer the crown to his grandson, the Duke of Bordeaux, as Henry V, while the representative of the Orléans branch would exercise a regency. These moves were all brushed aside in the face of threatened further insurrection. On August 3 the king, the last reigning French Bourbon, set out from Rambouillet for Cherbourg, and thence to exile in England.

### III   *The Making of a King*

That left open the issue of what new government the country would have. That issue, too, was promptly resolved, and in the resolution of it Thiers played as much as anyone the role of kingmaker. As fate would have it, just forty years later, he was to play a not dissimilar role. in French affairs, though on the later occasion, as we shall see, circumstances were vastly different and he himself would come into the executive succession. Thiers' role in the 1830 affair gives ample evidence of his determination and skill.

In the midst of the just-related events, what might be called a relic from the past, or a deus ex machina, appeared upon the scene. Lafayette was seventy-three years of age in 1830 and had been enjoying retirement surrounded by the aura of his American adventure and his initial support of the Revolution in France. Not a man of especially keen political acumen, his past record of consistent support of liberty and constitutionalism made him a symbol that could be used as a rallying point, possibly for a republican regime. Again the role of the municipality of Paris in the events of forty years before must be recalled, for it had been the backbone of the more radical aspects of the Great Revolution, largely responsible for the establishment of the first Republic in France. The current leadership, of whatever persuasion, would have no more of the Bourbons.

The conjunction of Thiers and Lafayette became crucial at this point, though there is no evidence of prior collusion between them; rather their actions in the midst of fluid circumstances complemented each other. The two men took essentially similar views of the situation and maneuvered to similar effect between the radical municipality and the less determined leadership that emerged from the Chamber, or at least that section of it that had been critical of the regime. Lafayette was not a priori opposed to a republic, but his memory of the course of events of forty years before, when he had felt he could no longer adhere to a tendency he considered excessive, made him fearful of a possible repetition of these same excesses.

Thiers was not adamantly antirepublican, but he felt that the French people were not ready for such a regime. He therefore remained a monarchist and his outlook may best be summed up in his own phrase, as he put it in the *National: Il nous faut cette république déguisée en monarchie* (we need this republic under the guise of a monarchy), a view not very different from that attributed to Lafayette, though subsequently denied by him: *la monarchie constitutionnelle, c'est la meilleure des républiques* (a constitutional monarchy is the best republic).

But Thiers was the chief mover, Lafayette being little more than an instrument in his hands, though an instrument used with consummate skill. Thiers was very active at this point and seemed to be everywhere. In the columns of his newspaper he had for some time been harping on the merits of the English model of 1688. A similar possibility was now open to France, which he strongly advocated. On the walls of Paris on the morning of July 30 the following manifesto appeared:

Charles X cannot come back to Paris: he has caused the blood of the people to be spilled.

The republic would cause horrible divisions among us and would embroil us with Europe.

The Duke of Orléans is a prince devoted to the cause of the Revolution.

The Duke of Orléans has never fought against us.

The Duke of Orléans was at Jemmapes.

The Duke of Orléans carried the tricolor banner under fire.

The Duke of Orléans has given his decision; he accepts the Charter as we have always wanted it.

He will hold his crown from the French people.[8]

The position Thiers was taking was the reverse, yet in a sense dictated by the same judgment as it would be forty years later. On the later occasion he would come to the conclusion that the Republic was the least divisive regime for the French; in 1830 he still saw the monarchy in that role. The reversal does not appear as inconsistency, but rather as the opposite, a realistic appraisal in both instances.

The just-cited manifesto, the work of Thiers and Mignet, implied that the consent of the Duke of Orléans had been acquired; there remained to be obtained that of the Hôtel de Ville. The first assertion was rather premature, the second part of the arrangement obviously an open question. In procuring both, Thiers was the puppeteer who maneuvered the strings.

The Duke of Orléans was not averse to assuming the crown. Son of the notorious Philippe Égalité who had even voted in the Con-

vention for the execution of Louis XVI, he had sufficient revolutionary credentials, but he was a cautious man and far from devoid of
intelligence. Thiers sought him out at Neuilly, but could only see
his able and politically shrewd sister, Madame Adelaïde, who con-
sented to use her influence to the desired effect.

The plan succeeded, aided by the consent of hesitant deputies, a
group reminiscent of the Convention's Plain. The compromise solution of asking the Duke of Orléans to assume the lieutenancy general of the kingdom, pending more definite and lasting arrangements, gave the duke a sufficient cover of legality. It was ostensibly
in response to the request of the deputies that he accepted, then
proceeded to issue a proclamation to the Parisians—the *Parisians*,
be it noted—closing with the seemingly innocuous statement that
"the Chamber will meet and decide upon the means to insure the
reign of law and the upholding of the rights of the nation. Henceforth the Charter will be a reality."[9]

There remained the second operation, the acceptance by the
Hôtel de Ville, a more delicate one, for among the municipality and
the people were those who suspected the intent behind what
seemed to them weasel words and who feared a sleight of hand that
would snatch from them the fruits of their victory. This is where
Lafayette's role became important. Following a meeting at the
Palais Royal of the duke and a rump of the Chamber (ninety-one
deputies), the duke wearing a tricolor badge and followed by the
deputies, set out on horseback for the Hôtel de Ville. The crowd
that watched the transit was of uncertain mood, and at the Hôtel de
Ville there was much argument and confusion. To make an involved
and picturesque story short, the issue was resolved when Lafayette
and the duke, wrapped in the tricolor flag, embraced each other on
the balcony of the Hôtel de Ville. To the emotional tableau the
crowd responded with shouts of *"Vive Lafayette! Vive le duc d'Orléans!"* The day had been carried. In one interpretation, the sleight
of hand had succeeded whereby the bourgeoisie had made use of
the revolutionary people of Paris for its own, limited ends.

The rest is a footnote that can just be mentioned for the sake of
completeness, without dwelling unduly on the legal details and aspects of the transfer of power. Guizot,[10] rather than Thiers, played
the leading role at this point. Charles X's abdication was registered,
but his appointment of the Duke of Orléans to his momentary succession was set aside, the throne being declared vacant. In theory

the Duke of Orléans was called upon to sit on the French throne, but certain modifications were effected in the 1814 Charter, with a view to curbing the possible use of arbitrary power.[11] These having been voted by the Chambers and accepted by the Duke of Orléans, his position was regularized. Significantly, in order to emphasize the break with the past and the source of his legitimacy, the new king would be Louis Philippe I—rather than Philippe VII—king of the French instead of king of France by the grace of God. He came into his functions on August 9 upon swearing allegiance to the modified Charter. The transformation had been almost entirely a Parisian affair, the rest of the country, little disturbed, acquiescing.

Although what had happened was mystifying to some, the republicans in particular, it is in retrospect quite clear. To contend that the revolution, the people, or radical Paris, had been bamboozled and betrayed is in a sense quite correct. But Thiers would have seen it otherwise. The monarchy of the Restoration had sought to abuse its power and the forces that opposed that abuse had been used to destroy it. But that did not mean that power should go to the volatile and incompetent mob—remember 1793—an element that Thiers feared and for which he had but contempt. Power should remain in the hands of a qualified élite, a small segment of society, the bourgeois, his own kind. This to him constituted no betrayal or treachery, but merely an intelligent direction of certain forces with a view to achieving sensible governance.

The word *élite* has fallen upon evil days. The current attacks upon it would have been difficult for Thiers to understand; for him a governing élite was a matter of course rather than a suitable object for discussion. It might as well be recognized for that matter that an élite is inescapable under any dispensation, though the composition of it can vary. In constitutionalism and the rights of man Thiers staunchly believed, but in the France of 1830 the sacred right of property still seemed, even to the liberals of the day, the simple and legitimate criterion for responsible position. Those who questioned that base, and there were some, were still few; seen in this light, the 1830 revolution and Thiers' preponderant role in that event may appear as no more than a step in the evolutionary trend of political progress.

CHAPTER 4

# Continued Progress in Politics

## I  *Character of the Regime*

DURING the period of the July Monarchy, especially the first decade of it, Thiers' activity was so closely intertwined with the political life of the country as to make the two inseparable stories. To the flattering observation, in the 1820s, that he would before long achieve ministerial rank, Thiers' reply was "I know it." Both the remark and the reply may have been banter, yet they also expressed a sound forecast.

Considering his role in procuring Louis Philippe's accession to the throne, his initial reward may have seemed disappointing. For, apart from membership in the Council of State, he had to be content with a relatively subordinate post in the ministry of finance, a position to which Baron Louis had called him. But Thiers was not inclined to bear grudges or nourish resentment; nor was he one to neglect the opportunities that even a secondary position might offer. Even allowing for membership in the Establishment of the day, his qualities of competence and capacity for hard work insured his attaining full ministerial rank within just over two years. He was minister of commerce and public works in 1833, more importantly minister of the interior a year later, while continuing in charge of public works as well. In February 1836, he would be in full command as prime minister.

Thiers was fully satisfied with the outcome of the 1830 revolution, but there were those in France who were not: the Legitimists, who looked upon the son of regicide Philippe Égalité as a usurper; more radically inclined republicans, the Parisian workers who had manned the barricades and not unjustifiably felt that they had been used as tools in a maneuver skillfully directed by others. We shall presently see how Thiers dealt with both tendencies. As to Bonapartists, despite the prosperity of the Napoleonic legend, they did not constitute a significant group, and the death of Napoleon's heir, the Duke of Reichstadt, in 1832 further enfeebled their cause.

The chief concern of the new regime was to achieve the legitimacy of acceptance, at home no less than abroad. At home two main tendencies manifested themselves. What has been called the party of resistance was made up of those who, like Thiers himself, were satisfied with the current outcome and wished to operate the country, under the somewhat modified Charter, as a constitutional monarchy on the English model. Opposed to it was the party of movement, those who regarded the change as a first step along the path of further transformation, republicans for the most part. These, it should be remembered, are characterizations of broad tendencies, not of organized political parties as we know them today.

There was in addition the problem of the king himself and of his own views of his role. Louis Philippe was not a fighting man and the picture of him that has come down to us is more commonly associated with the caricatures of Daumier. This is somewhat of a distortion, for Louis Philippe, bourgeois as his state and his own tastes may have been, was not devoid of intelligence, skill, or finesse. Though respectful of the constitution, he was highly desirous of asserting his ruling prerogative and ever sought to exert influence in the choice of his ministers. He could even on occasion take a determined stand, his confrontation with Thiers in 1840[1] being the best example of that capability.

The new regime needed the sanction of popular endorsement, elections, and for holders of governmental office it was desirable to hold the rank of deputy as well. Thiers presented himself in his home ground of Aix where he was duly elected in October, and he continued to represent this constituency throughout the period of the July Monarchy. It is important to bear in mind the minuscule size of the electorate at this time, a little over 200,000 in a country of thirty million, the franchise being based on property qualifications, which were still higher when it came to eligibility. Thiers himself did not possess sufficient property, but the matter was rectified through his purchase of a house in Paris. The deal was arranged through connections, that of Madame Dosne in particular, whose husband was in real estate and many other types of business. More will have to be said about the somewhat unusual relationship between Thiers and the Dosne family.

The first half of the decade of the 1830s, where the new regime was concerned, was a period of consolidation, of securing recognition both at home and abroad. The banker Laffitte, Casimir Périer, the Duc de Broglie, Marshal Soult, headed the ministry at various times, though they were not necessarily the directing personalities of their respective administrations. It would exceed the bounds of this treatment to follow the vicissitudes of these administrations; it is Thiers' role in them and in the Chamber, as well as some of his private affairs, on which we wish to focus.

## II   *Thiers in Parliament and in Office*

His first performance in the Chamber of Deputies was hardly a success. His diminutive stature, the quality of his delivery and of his voice combined to make a poor impression. But he soon learned and before long acquired the reputation of an orator, always master of his subject, even when resorting to improvisation, which he not infrequently did. Some working class agitation in 1831 was promptly repressed and the subsequent ministry of Casimir Périer was of conservative orientation.[2]

In the discussion of the reply to the address from the throne Thiers undertook a spirited defense of the regime. A passage of his speech may be quoted as descriptive of his orientation and outlook at this point:

The commitment of the July revolution was to not repeat the revolution of 1789 and its excesses. . . . That commitment . . . has guided all its [the government's] actions. It is with this in mind that, from the beginning, instead of instituting a republic, the monarchy has been maintained; it is with this thought that, instead of abusing the vanquished, it has given them the benefits of the law; it is with this thought that, instead of renewing conquests and invasions, it has tried to keep the peace so long as that could be done with honor.[3]

And again on a later occasion:

What happened to them [the Convention of 1793]? That which happens when one departs from truth, that which happens when the lawgiver is untrue to the time, the customs, reality; they made laws that were only a dream: lie was followed by a striking denial. The Directory through its disorder, its unchecked debauchery, its dilapidations, was a sad and scandalous denial of that austerity and a mere excess of barbarism. . . . It became necessary for a great man, as sensible as he was great, to put an end to that confusion.[4]

Or, in another form, in the course of commenting on republican agitation: "Representative monarchy is the best republic."[5]

The Casimir Périer ministry came to an end when its head fell victim to the cholera epidemic in May 1832. Shortly thereafter the government was confronted with an odd situation. The Duchess of Berry, widow of Charles X's son, entered France from Italy and betook herself to the Vendée in the hope of provoking a rising in favor of her son, the Legitimist pretender, the Duke of Chambord, in that strongly Royalist region. She found little response and was arrested in her hiding place in Nantes. Her giving birth to a daughter while in prison cast ridicule upon her cause that emerged discredited from the incident. She was conveniently allowed to depart, thus avoiding the awkwardness of a trial, a course defended in the Chamber by Thiers, who was largely responsible for her apprehension, then release.[6]

Thiers was a member of the ministry, of which, together with Guizot, he constituted the backbone; the two could still agree at this time on their support of Louis Philippe's rule. Guizot was responsible for the noted education law, a matter in which Thiers played little part. A measure of Thiers' liberalism, if such it can be called, may be seen in his opposition to an enlargement of the electorate, a proposal against which he spoke in the Chamber in January. This was consistent with the importance he attached to the criterion of property, and he was likewise opposed to the introduction of an income tax.

He took a lively interest in finance and economic activity, domains of which he had a solid grasp, but he was cautious in the matter of protection, a subject on which he expressed himself as follows:

The world of today has embarked upon novel paths. All peoples wish to be closer to each other, to expand, to exchange their products. An attempt is made to replace total barriers by tariffs, high tariffs with lower ones. France will not be the last to follow that example. But, while adopting a new and broader system, whose aim is the progressive liberation of industries, the government must declare that it wishes to proceed with prudence and gradualness. . . . It [the government] knows one authority alone, experience. . . . All who have studied and reflected acknowledge that in no country and at no time can one find a serious and solid good that has been accomplished with suddenness.[7]

On a visit to England, where his fame had preceded him, Thiers was well received and entertained and he made careful observation of the operation of a government that he always looked upon as a model, as well as of the economic development of the country. But he did not sufficiently realize the importance of railways though he acknowledged the inevitability of their growth.

In his supervision of public works he took considerable interest in that domain of his competence, arguing that the state alone could undertake certain projects, whether in the capital or in the provinces. Thiers has been properly regarded as an exponent of French nationalism. A nice expression of that feeling is reported by Nassau Senior:

> What a nation is France! How mistaken in her objects, how absurd in her means, yet how glorious is the result of her influence and of her example! I do not say that we are a happy people; I do not say that we are good neighbors; we are always in hot water ourselves, and we are always the pest and the plague of all who have anything to do with us, but after all we are the salt of the earth. We are always fighting, always inquiring, always inventing, always destroying prejudices, and breaking up institutions, and supplying political science with new facts, new experiments, and new warnings. Two or three thousand years hence, when civilization has passed on in its western course, when Europe is in the state we now see Asia Minor and Syria and Egypt, only two of her children will be remembered. One a sober well-disposed good boy, the other a riotous unmanageable spoilt child, and I am not sure that posterity will not like the naughty boy better.[8]

The statue of Napoleon atop the column of the Place Vendôme had been taken down by the Restoration. Putting it up again in July 1833 was the occasion for a ceremony characterized by colorful pomp, military as well as civilian, in which Thiers proudly took part in the full regalia of his office. To his interest in history his *History of the French Revolution* bore witness; the lively and enthusiastic description in that work of Napoleon's first Italian campaign, for example, conveyed his appreciative response to French military accomplishments. In a less bellicose vein, the foundation in 1833 of the *Société d'histoire de France*, in which he shared with Guizot,

Mignet, and others, may also be regarded as evidence of an interest where scholarship went hand in hand with the sense of national pride.

### III  *Foreign Affairs*

But from this nationalistic feeling it would be a mistake to think of Thiers as entertaining aggressive intent. That Parisian events would have European repercussions he fully appreciated, but far from his thoughts was any desire to revive the crusading ardor of the Convention. The constitution of 1791 was closer to his conception of proper governance, the type of social ordering that he wished Louis Philippe to consolidate in the country. For the rest he agreed with the new king in the latter's desire to avoid alarming Europe and to convince the powers of France's wholly peaceful intent. This is a good place to examine Thiers' views and his role in a number of issues of foreign policy, especially as this is a domain in which he was to play a major role on subsequent occasions as well.

### *The Problem of Belgium*

The news of the Parisian revolution did indeed stir Europe, and hope again rose high in liberal hearts throughout much of the continent. A concrete and potentially dangerous issue almost immediately arose in neighboring Belgium.

The settlement of 1815 had joined that land with Holland under the rule of the Dutch king, in part compensation for Holland's overseas losses to England, while Austria relinquished the possession of it in exchange for the Italian Lombardo-Venetian kingdom. But the people of the former Austrian Netherlands, though ethnically divided between Flemings and French-speaking Walloons, were united in their dislike of what seemed to them rather heavy-handed alien Dutch rule. Also they were Catholic in the main, though with a strong admixture among the Walloons of eighteenth-century Voltairean, hence in the context of the day liberal, outlook.

Within one month of the Parisian revolution there was a rising in Brussels, from which Dutch forces were expelled. The inadequate and belated concessions of King William IV and his failure to suppress the rising resulted in October in a Belgian declaration of independence. A mere fifteen years after the defeat of Napoleon's France here was undoubtedly a modification of the order established at Vienna. It raised the question of what the powers would do in response to the Dutch king's appeal for assistance against the challenge to his legitimate rule.

The Tsar's response was the most enthusiastic, and he would have sent help had he not been so far away and involved in similarly liberal nationalistic agitation in his own Polish domain. Metternich, more concerned with Italian affairs, was halfhearted, as was also the Prussian king, where Belgium was concerned. The crucial question was whether France would assist the Belgian rebellion, an action that had advocates in France. But such action would have run into British opposition, with the consequence that the issue of war or peace lay in Paris and London.

To the latter capital, even before the Belgian rising, Talleyrand had been sent as ambassador. The old man—he was seventy-six at this time—has been and is a controversial figure. Napoleon's vulgarly terse appraisal, *de la merde dans un bas de soie* (ordure wrapped up in a silk stocking), may be recalled, as well as Chateaubriand's judgment, "for money Talleyrand would sell his soul—and he would be right, for he would be trading muck for gold." However, Talleyrand by this time had become something of a legend and his diplomatic skill was universally acknowledged. It would be difficult to deny that, for all that he had done extremely well for himself in the process, Talleyrand had consistently served the French interest, a fact erected by some into the fundamental principle of his diplomacy.

The significance of his British mission was that France wanted peace, a fact of which he soon convinced the British government. That accomplished, a convergence of British and French views was achieved, for the British had no particular feelings about the sanctity of the international of rulers, nor could they become exercised over the grant of constitutions, in Paris, in Brussels or elsewhere. France having taken the position that she would not intervene in Belgium, provided only that no one else did, the outcome, sanctioned at an international conference in London, was the acknowledgment by the powers of the independence of Belgium, a result essentially accomplished by the end of the year.[9] Palmerston, who had come to the foreign office in November, was satisfied with what he considered adequate guarantees against the spread of French influence in Belgium. A measure of the degree of Anglo-French agreement may be seen in the fact that in 1831 a French army went into Belgium to repel a Dutch attempt at reestablishing control, and in 1832 Anglo-French naval action worked to the same effect. More will have to be said about this Anglo-French cooperation, that Thiers would exaggeratedly characterize as an alliance.

### Poland and Italy

Tsar Nicholas, as mentioned before, was confronted with rebellion in Poland. The eighteenth-century destruction of that state and its division among its three neighbors had been confirmed at Vienna in 1815. But although Russian Poland enjoyed a special status and even had a constitution of its own, Polish national feeling remained dissatisfied. The July revolution in Paris found an echo in Warsaw, but order was eventually restored in Poland, made as a consequence into essentially another Russian province.

Franco-Polish relations had a long background, and for a time the Duchy of Warsaw had existed as a Napoleonic creation. In addition, there were those in France, liberals of republican inclination, still imbued with the crusading spirit of the Revolution, who would have assisted freedom-seeking Poles as well as Belgians. But Warsaw is farther away from Paris than Brussels, and in view of what we have just seen of the French behavior in the Belgian case there was little likelihood that any action would be taken in the Polish, even apart from the incomparably greater logistical difficulty. Sympathy was expressed in France for the Polish rebellion, even in the Chamber, where Sébastiani's phrase—he was foreign minister at the time—"order reigns in Warsaw" aroused angry criticism. But this French reticence did not even go very far in changing the Tsar's poor opinion of French political ways and of the new king of the French.

In Italy as well, national sentiment and liberal desires commanded an appreciable following. Their suppression in 1820 has been mentioned. They manifested themselves in the central part of the peninsula, Parma, Modena, and the Papal States, again sparked to a point by the Parisian events. Italy is a neighbor of France, but most of it was Metternich's domain, and once again Austrian troops appeared in Bologna. The French response to this Austrian action was ambivalent; no help was given to the Italian insurrection, but a French force was sent to occupy Ancona, on the pretext, however, of balance of power considerations, to match the Austrian intrusion.

One is reminded of Talleyrand's characterization of intervention and nonintervention as two doctrines that have fundamentally the same meaning.

Thiers' reaction to these events can be found in the speech he delivered in the Chamber on March 6, 1832 in connection with the debate on the foreign affairs appropriation, in response to attacks on what was described as the reticent timidity of French policy. Thiers staunchly defended that policy, asserting that the new French regime constituted a return to the proper aims of the Revolution, but was equally opposed to war against all Europe, a likely consequence of intervention anywhere.

In Belgium especially, such an intervention would have aroused the same British opposition to suspected French annexationist designs as forty years earlier. Instead of this, an Anglo-French alliance had come into existence, certainly cooperation that had made possible Belgian independence without general war. France had thus peacefully reaped the very substantial benefit of the destruction of the Netherlandish kingdom, in large part an anti-French creation.[10]

Where Poland was concerned, while expressing sympathy for the Polish desire for liberty, Thiers defended the principle of nonintervention, largely on correct grounds of geography and of the limitations of French power, more speciously on the basis of the Tsar's constitutional position in Poland.

Thiers' position in the Italian case deserves special attention in the light of later—during the Second Empire—developments in the peninsula. Addressing the critics of the refusal to give assistance to the liberal forces in both Poland and Italy, he had this to say:

Just as the government would have been saddled with the obligation to make Poland, so likewise it would have been confronted with the problem, insoluble today, of making Italy.

Enlarging on the condition of Italy, he went on:

Those are the difficulties that caused Napoleon to say that it would take centuries, or at least a great many years, before Italy would achieve the maturity that makes possible constitutional institutions, and the homogeneity that makes possible a unitary government.

On the other hand he defined the nature of the French interest in Italy:

> I say that we could not allow the fate of Italy to be decided by a single power, that we had to intervene there, that our action in Italy does not contravene our political principles any more than did our going into Belgium to prevent a counter revolution.

But on the score of foreign policy in general he stressed again the importance of the English factor:

> There is one war that France must always fear, however brave and strong she may be, and it is a war with all Europe, including England.[11]

In regard to the English connection he had also this to say on a somewhat later occasion:

> When there was a liberal, a national, government, in England for example, France found a noble ally who had shed old prejudices in order to effect a rapprochement with her, and let herself be guided by the sympathies that our revolution inspired.[12]

Thiers' view of the English connection was unwarrantedly sanguine, or at least premature, for the convergence of the interests of the two countries did not become a reality until the end of the century, after Thiers was gone, and the realization of it in the form of solid cooperation, on the English side in particular, did not take place, and in very hesitant fashion at that, until the opening decade of the twentieth century.[13]

There was point nevertheless in stressing the affinity between the two regimes. In the context of the day, when constitution was the great shibboleth and hope of all that was liberal, Britain and France did indeed both represent the liberal tendency of the future, certainly in contrast with the absolutist regimes that still prevailed in Austria, Prussia, and Russia. But Britain had no desire to launch upon a crusade in defense of representative institutions anywhere, and the France of Louis Philippe was similarly averse to fighting outside her borders for the sake of the rights of man. Yet, to repeat, if the ideological affinity between the institutions of the two countries did in certain respects and on specific occasions facilitate the cooperative conjunction of positions, the more important aspect of their relations was still that of their centuries-old rivalry.

### Mediterranean Issues

In the Mediterranean, Britain and France (and Russia) had worked together in procuring the emergence of an independent small kingdom of Greece.[14] But, more generally, the two countries felt the same interest in resisting the Russian expansionist urge at the Straits and beyond. There is no room to go into the complexity of Ottoman affairs; let it suffice to say that the rise of an able vassal of the Sultan in Egypt led to open conflct between the vassal and the suzerain. In 1833 the Sultan's forces fared poorly against the Egyptians in Syria.

It was Russian intervention that saved the Sultan at this point, in the form of an alliance, a pact of mutual assistance, which, like all such combinations between unequal powers, was tantamount to the weaker being put in the position of protected dependent. There was no immediate British or French reaction to the success of Russian diplomacy that was the Treaty of Unkiar Skelessi. But at the other end of the Mediterranean, in Spain, the death of King Ferdinand opened the issue of his succession. His attempt to secure the throne for his young daughter, while his widow would hold the regency, was not accepted by his brother Don Carlos, and Spain was torn by the Carlist war. A somewhat similar situation had arisen in Portugal, following the death of the king in 1826.

The result of these Iberian complications was what has been called the Quadruple Alliance, a combination in which both Britain and France joined in support of the "legitimate" holders of the Spanish and Portuguese crowns respectively, Britain and France both throwing the weight of their influence in favor of the liberal forces in the Iberian peninsula. The fact that the Austro-Russian Convention of Münschengrätz bespoke another understanding between those conservative powers emphasized the cleavage of Europe between the conservative and the liberal camps. It is of interest to juxtapose some dates: the Russo-Turkish agreement was in June 1833, the Austro-Russian in September, the Quadruple Alliance dated from the following April.

That the characterization of first Entente Cordiale to describe this arrangement was premature has been indicated. Thiers was enthusiastically in favor of it and defended it in the Chamber on more than one occasion, his only criticism being of the French refusal of outright intervention in Spain, where the Foreign Legion alone was allowed to operate.

CHAPTER 5

# A More Conservative Orientation

THE year 1833 was an eventful one for Thiers. The foundation of the *Société d'histoire de France* has been mentioned. In June he became a member of the French Academy, an acknowledgment of his literary accomplishments, even if one allow for the normal intrigues of the French literary and political worlds. The occasion of his reception was a brilliant affair, attended by the lights of Parisian society, literary and political, including aged Talleyrand who hobbled to it to hear his protégé perform. Thiers' speech, in duly polished style, paid the customary homage to his not overdistinguished predecessor, and though, as he himself said, "I am here not before a political assembly but before an academy," he could not resist the temptation to introduce the subject close to his heart, the Great Revolution, which, to be sure, he did in measured philosophical language.

A few months later, in December, he was married to a much younger woman who might have been his daughter, 16-year-old Elise Dosne, an arrangement that gave rise to some very unkind gossip. Thiers had long been familiar with the Dosne household, his most intimate connection being Mme Dosne; he was involved as well in profitable business transactions through her husband, the above-mentioned purchase of a house before the 1830 election, for example.

As time passed and M. Dosne was increasingly absent from Paris, filling administrative posts in the provinces, in the appointment to which Thiers was often to have a hand in his ministerial capacity, the Thiers household in Paris came to consist of himself and his three ladies, his wife, her sister, and his mother-in-law, a situation that came to be increasingly accepted in Parisian social arrangements. The management of the household was more in Mme Dosne's than in Mme Thiers' hands—the latter's very young age might have

52

explained this at first. It was, to say the least, a very odd ménage, inevitably the butt of gossip. We shall be content with what may seem the unexciting observation that Thiers seems to have been a normal heterosexual man and that the meaningful aspect of his activity, political and literary, remained essentially unaffected by his love or sexual life. Having said this, in full awareness of deliberate but justified limitation, we may proceed to follow Thiers' public career.

## I  The Social Question

The ministry of Casimir Périer had represented a generally conservative orientation, quite acceptable to the king. After Périer's death, a victim of the cholera epidemic, in May 1832, there was a period of hesitancy in the government until a ministry was organized in October, headed by Marshal Soult. This lasted until July 1834. Soult himself counted for less than either Thiers or Guizot, who at this time could still agree on the general direction of policy, though differences in their respective styles at least could already be perceived. Louis Philippe himself was anxious to assert his own control of his ministers, a tendency that raised the constitutional issue of the precise locus of ultimate power.

But Thiers could still defend the action of the government, and a measure of his liberalism, or the opposite in another interpretation, may be seen in the fact that he spoke in the Chamber in January 1833 in opposition to an enlargement of the electorate,[1] an issue that arose in connection with the forthcoming election that was to take place in June. In his view the error of the French Revolution was to have attempted too much change too fast; the July Monarchy would not repeat that mistake, and control must remain in the hands of the qualified few. As he put it at the end of the following year: "I am a minister of the July government for the purpose of resisting the revolution when it threatens to go astray."[2]

By that time certain things had happened that indeed gave point to that statement. Thiers' picture of the state of the country as one of peace and prosperity was unwarrantedly rosy and about to be belied at the very moment he so represented it in the discussion of the reply to the address from the throne.[3]

It was in February that labor trouble developed among the silk workers of Lyons. The strike that ensued did not last, but the fact that it had taken place at all was cause for alarm. One reaction was to propose legislation to strengthen the existing law, too easily circumvented, that would have restricted the right of association to groups of twenty members. In effect this was an early instance of the debate of the right of labor to organize. Thiers helped defeat amendments to the further restriction of the right of association.

In Lyons itself there were protests, political on the part of the local section of the Society of the Rights of Man, social on the part of the workers, six of whose leaders were to be tried. The trial, set in April, sparked four days of violent rioting that the government used as an occasion to give a demonstration of its firmness. The plan was immediately successful, but there were repercussions elsewhere in the country, notably in Paris. The government, Thiers in particular, believed, or pretended to believe, that insurrectionist attempts were the work of anarchist machinations, and was determined to assert its authority in exemplary fashion. A large concentration of troops had little difficulty in reestablishing order in the east central quarters of the city, focus of the insurrection, to the accompaniment of considerable brutality, a normal aspect of such performances. The Parisian "massacre of the rue Transnonain" has been perpetuated by Daumier.

Thiers had no hesitancy in defending the repression, about which he had this to say in the Chamber:

> I know that it is popular today to cast dishonor upon civil war, to criticize the shedding of French blood, and this is undoubtedly justified. But note well that the blame is bitterly directed against the defenders of public order, and very gentle for those who attack it; civil war is looked upon as dishonorable, but for those who defend the law, not for those who attack it.
>
> Rewards have been given to our brave soldiers who have risked their lives for the sake of public order . . . and who have well deserved the decorations given them. There is an attempt to tarnish these decorations, because they are placed on the breasts of those who have fought against anarchy.[4]

The defense of law and order ever remains the first care of any regime, even a revolutionary one that has succeeded in overthrowing the anteceding legality. It is also the pretext commonly used by the holders of power, whether grievances against the established order are justified or not. Contending that the workers were misled by anarchist agitators was not in 1834 very convincing, and the episode just recounted brings to mind a preview of what Thiers was to do in Paris in 1871, a much larger affair of which more will be said in later pages.[5]

It would take us too far afield to enter into the details of ministerial reshufflings that filled the better part of a year, an experience familiar in France under the Third Republic which the French word *bafouillage* (confused mumbling) aptly describes. The central issue at this time was still that of who should govern, the king or the legislature. Louis Philippe desired to rule as well as to reign, but even the Chamber issued from a minuscule electorate was jealous of its prerogative. On that issue, though Thiers would serve the king and they got along well enough with each other, sometimes to the accompaniment of reciprocal quips, Thiers was a staunch and consistent adherent of the English model: the king should reign but not rule.

But he also remained a resolute defender of order against the pretensions of the incompetent and fickle mob. His above-cited speech of May 12, 1834 is worth reading in full as an eloquent exposition of what, in the context of the day, could be described as enlightened conservatism. In that speech he raised the fundamental question, one still very much alive in our day, of the extent to which concessions can be made, of the manner in which social change can and should be implemented. Change he would not deny, not even the legitimacy of violence in certain situations, and the responsibility of the *beati possidentes* for adaptation to changing circumstances. Was he not after all the defender of the initial revolution in France? To be sure, he had now himself joined the ranks of these *beati possidentes*, a fact that had appreciable effect in coloring his perception.

The same position he had occasion to assert again in March 1835, in connection with the aftermath of the insurrectionary events of the preceding year. The governmental fumbling was finally resolved when Louis Philippe was forced to accept a ministry headed by the Duc de Broglie despite his personal dislike of the man. Earlier, in 1834, the government had sought indemnification for the victims of the Lyons troubles, attempting to make a distinction between the innocent sufferers of the damage inflicted and those responsible for the rising. Thiers spoke in favor of the proposal[6] but the Chamber refused its consent. The matter came up again a year later. Thiers, now minister of the interior, took the same position in a speech[7] that brought out with great clarity precisely where he stood on the social question: a reasonable willingness to compromise with the demands for legitimate change combined with total intransigence vis-à-vis dangerous troublemakers.

Thus he defended the propriety of the trial and of the sentencing of the leaders of the 1834 troubles. The trial took place during most of the year 1835 before the upper house, the Chamber of Peers, rather than before an ordinary tribunal, and was a good barometer of the temper of the country and of the strength of the controlling forces in it. In Paris there was appreciable sympathy for the accused who endeavored to use the proceedings as a platform from which to indict the regime. There were disorderly scenes in the court but the final outcome was a severe setback to the republican leadership. The regime was consolidating itself on a conservative basis, a tendency that would eventually result in the rift between Thiers and Guizot, though they did not part company at this point. This veering toward the right on the part of the regime could be observed as well in the domain of foreign policy, as we shall presently see. Metternich was becoming more attractive to Louis Philippe than the ostensibly more ideologically kindred British regime. But we must not anticipate our story. Thiers at this time still supported the repressive tendency of the day, as evidenced by his position in the matter of attempts to introduce restrictions on the freedom of the press. That attempt received a fillip from another incident that occurred the same year.

The anniversary of the 1830 revolution, the *trois glorieuses*, had been an annual celebration. On the way from the Church of the Madeleine to the Bastille the royal procession was greeted by a terrible explosion that caused a large number of casualties in the immediate entourage of the king, who, however, emerged unscathed, as did also Thiers. The attempted assassination had failed and in fact it immediately redounded to the popularity of the king who had behaved with exemplary coolness. The deed came as no special surprise to Thiers who, in his ministerial capacity, had had police warning of it;[8] the effect of it, in combination with the unrest of the preceding year, was to accentuate the repressive tendency of the government. It was proposed to institute curbs on a very free press through prior censorship of publication, a measure that Thiers defended in the Chamber.[9] His view of things was colored by his official capacity, though he might have been reminded of his own words on the subject on the score of the policy of the Directory:

> Though well used to freedom, it [the Directory] was alarmed by the language that was used in certain newspapers; it did not yet sufficiently understand that anything must be allowed to be said, that lies are never to be feared, however publicized they may be, that their very violence wears them out, and that truth alone can cause a government to perish, especially suppressed truth. It asked both houses to enact laws curbing the abuses of the press.[10]

## II *Thiers' First Prime Ministership, February–September 1836*

Tranquillity seemed assured in the country under the guidance of the triumvirate of Broglie, Thiers, and Guizot, despite the dislike of the king for his prime minister and of certain foreign policy divergences on the score of the English connection in particular. The address from the throne and the Chamber's reply to it passed as little more than formalities, when, unexpectedly, an unfavorable vote in January on a minor budgetary matter resulted in the fall of the ministry that no one seemed to regret. The door was open for Thiers' assumption of the prime ministership, to which he was called by the king.

### American Interlude

Before considering his rather brief tenure of the office, from February to September 1836, a digression is indicated which holds special interest for the American reader and the student of Franco-American relations.

As a consequence of the Napoleonic wars and in connection with the economic warfare of which the emperor's Berlin and Milan decrees were expression, the United States had entered claims against France for damages sustained from the seizure of American ships. The validity of the American claim was acknowledged by France, but the fall of Napoleon had left the issue pending. It had been taken up again during the Restoration, a compromise agreement being finally reached, when that regime in turn had fallen. In January 1831 a treaty was signed at last between the two countries, setting the American claim at twenty-five million francs. The ministry of Marshal Soult got around to submitting the treaty for ratifica-

tion in April 1834. The rejection of it by a small majority of the
Chamber resulted in a reshuffling of the ministry; the Duc de Broglie, feeling personally involved in his capacity of foreign minister,
resigned and this was the occasion on which Thiers entered the
ministry as minister of the interior. Matters were not helped by the
proposal of The President of the United States, Andrew Johnson,
that Congress take retaliatory action, and when the discussion of the
American debt was resumed it fell to Thiers on two occasions, on
April 9 and 16, to reply in close argumentation to the attacks against
the treaty. The matter was finally settled with the endorsement of a
ratifying resolution by a more than two to one majority. Thiers had
carried conviction.

We are tempted to draw a parallel with another debate of a comparable nature when, in December 1932, the problem of the debt to
the United States resulting from the first World War was debated in
the French parliament. The government of Edouard Herriot argued
the legitimacy of the debt, but parliament disagreed and the government fell. In the latter case the problem was never settled save
by default. It is an interesting reflection that of the major European
states, with only two, Russia and France, has the United States
never engaged in open hostilities. This is no place to comment on
the state of Russo-American relations, but in the case of those between the United States and its oldest ally they have been for two
centuries characterized by notable ups and downs and perhaps an
unusual amount of emotional content. The episodes just indicated
are illustrations.

We may now return to the period of Thiers' first tenure of the
prime ministership. Like his subsequent one four years later, it was
of brief duration and came to an end over foreign policy questions,
Thiers in both instances holding the foreign office portfolio as well as
the prime ministership.

Where domestic matters were concerned, Thiers' policy had no
marked orientation. The generally conciliatory address from the
throne, stressing the state of domestic peace, did not give rise to
sharp debate. On two occasions, in April and in May, Thiers dis-
coursed on the subject of tariffs. While arguing for their flexibility,
he took a generally protectionist stand, on the usual plea of the need
to shelter infant industries. Interestingly, especially in view of later
developments, he took the sensible enough view that the Zollverein

was a natural association, one which France could not in any way
have prevented, but he badly misjudged in asserting that it had no
political implications. As he would put it again somewhat later: "The
Prussian customs union is a temporary convenience; at the first
movement of an army the customs union will disintegrate."[11] There
will be occasion to discuss his great speech of 1866 on the trend of
German affairs.[12]

A very long speech in May on the subject of credits for the
monuments of the capital and another two weeks later on subsidies
for the theater testified to his interest in matters cultural and to his
already mentioned mastery of detail. In June he painted a highly
favorable picture of the financial management of the regime since its
inception.[13]

### The First Entente Cordiale

But foreign policy mattered more. At the beginning of June he
made several speeches that together furnish a comprehensive outline of his orientation. The point has been made before that Thiers
was an advocate of Anglo-French cooperation. Having surveyed the
general position of France at the outset of the existing regime in
these words:

> Our alliances have been based on this broad conception, to safeguard the
> July revolution through the preservation of peace, to consolidate the great-
> ness of France also through peace, and to foster gradual and peaceful de-
> velopment, always in peace. There, I insist, lay the motivation of our al-
> liances.
> It is with this thought that the government surveyed Europe. We can
> acknowledge today that a favorable condition has taken the place of that
> which initially existed. What impressed us at first was the general suspicion
> toward France: it was inevitable. Suspicion could not help but be the reac-
> tion to that revolution which had begun by upsetting a throne, though, to
> be sure, this was only done because there was no alternative, . . .

he went on to explain the advantages that derived from cooperation
with England:

> Clearly if England and France were in accord war was impossible; the
> first conquest to be accomplished in the promotion of peace was therefore
> that of the English people. Recall the record of the last forty years: which
> are the forces that made the war so prolonged and so harsh in all Europe?

They are on the one hand the inexhaustible armies of France, on the other the inexhaustible financial resources of England.

It is clear that if the armies of France were joined to the financial power of England no war was possible; that is the large idea which led to the English alliance.[14]

And this, he claimed, had been achieved, in part because of the change that had taken place in the English perception of France in the recent past, a change that he had himself been able to observe during his visit to England.

There was more along the same lines the following day when he reviewed the various problems in which French interests had been involved, and a week later he defended the policy of penetration in Algeria instead of being content with the control of coastal points.[15] He repeated this in July before the upper house,[16] between the two occasions sketching a favorable view of the handling of finances since 1830.[17] As he put it, the ultimate purpose of war is the establishment of peace, but that could only be secured in Algeria by moving into the interior.

It is normal for any administration to paint its management in favorable colors. There is no denying that from the first, in the Belgian situation, for example, and somewhat later in Spain, Thiers had staunchly believed in the desirability and the advantages of Anglo-French cooperation. But there was also point in the criticism of those who were sceptical of the solidity of the connection, not so much on the classical score of British duplicity as because of the very real and well-established tradition of Anglo-French rivalry and difference.

Without seeking to apportion blame for its demise, a possibly interesting but futile exercise, the fact remains that the first Entente Cordiale was a fragile affair and a premature description of a relationship that at this time had no substantial roots. There was more to the divergence, which grew out of the fact that the French king, behind his cautious constitutional behavior, was anxious to rule as well as to reign, and in fact was inclined to seek the support of the conservative courts, of Metternich in particular.

In any case Anglo-French relations cooled and French suspicions were fully reciprocated across the Channel, by such as Palmerston, a man often not restrained by the niceties of diplomatic intercourse.[18] Old Talleyrand himself, the architect as much as any one of the Anglo-French community of views over Belgium and Greece, was feeling disillusioned. As he put it to Louis Philippe:

> What can your Majesty still expect from England? We have exploited her alliance from which no more advantages are to be derived. It is owing to our alliance with England that peace has been preserved; now it can only offer us revolutions. Your Majesty's interest therefore required it to seek a rapprochement with the eastern powers. . . . The great courts do not like you, but they are beginning to have respect for you.[19]

And despite his ostensible defense of the English alliance Thiers himself was not really averse to such a reorientation, at least as a tactical move. The position he took in putting pressure on the federal government of Switzerland to procure the eviction of liberal agitators earned Austrian and Russian commendation, and it was consistent to entertain the possibility that a union between the French ruling house and the Austrian would add the stamp of respectability to the former.

The project of a marriage between a French prince and an Austrian princess was not Thiers' own nor was it new, but he took interest in it and a visit of two of Louis Philippe's sons, the Dukes of Orléans and of Nemours, to Berlin and Vienna was arranged. They were well received and made a good impression at the Viennese court, but Metternich, on whom the final decision depended, especially in view of the emperor's near-imbecilic condition, was hesitant; it was difficult to forget the recent fate of the Austrian princesses, Marie Antoinette and Marie Louise, who had married into the reigning houses of France. His final decision was unfavorable, a decision to which another attempt on the life of Louis Philippe, in June 1836, may have contributed; life among the French royal family did not after all seem very safe.

This last attempt also contributed to the subdued atmosphere in which the inauguration of the Arc de Triomphe took place the following month. The construction of that monument to Napoleonic glory, understandably delayed during the Restoration, had finally been completed. The memorial held considerable appeal to the French sense of glory, and the plan was at first to make the inauguration an occasion for the annual celebration of the three glorious days of July 1830. Louis Philippe was very desirous of presiding at the ceremony, but, concerned for his safety and pretexting the wish not to irritate foreign governments, his ministers, Thiers included, induced him to abandon the scheme. The inauguration took place in rather muted fashion, presided over by Thiers, who was after all the head of the government.

Metternich's rebuff over the marriage proposal had annoyed him and he thought to have found a suitable ground for a counterrebuff in Spain. In that country the Carlist war still went on and the government of the regent, Maria Cristina, was appealing to France for assistance in the form of armed forces. Thiers was now willing to send to Spain a corps of volunteers under the leadership of Marshal Bugeaud of Algerian fame. But he ran into the determined veto of the king, who was loath to risk Metternich's displeasure, not to mention that of Palmerston, ever suspicious of the prospect of a substantial French contingent in the peninsula. When Thiers offered his resignation, perhaps somewhat to his surprise it was accepted and his first prime ministership came to an end.

Louis Philippe was quietly pursuing the policy of establishing his own rule. Thiers was for him too strong a personality and the king seized the occasion to rid himself of his too-domineering minister. Louis Philippe was not reticent of confidences with foreign ambassadors; to the Prussian he had this to say: "Beg your king to consider, in judging me, the difficulty of my position. . . . I have had to endure Thiers for six months in order to show France his worth."[20] The dismissal of Thiers was highly approved among the conservative courts. He had, over a period, certainly served the king well, but the relations between the two were characterized by a curious combination of reciprocal respect and esteem with equally reciprocal contempt and dislike.

### III   An Interim, 1836–1840

The king had had his way; the outward manifestation of the assertion of his personal role in governmental councils was the succeeding ministry, headed by Molé, the king's man, a ministry that lasted for three years. Guizot accepted a position in the new cabinet, but was eliminated by March, while the country was entering a period of unexciting mediocrity during which the regime seemed to be achieving increasing stability. The attempt, in October 1836, of the heir to the Napoleonic claim to provoke a rising in the Strasbourg garrison ended in ridicule that only showed the weakness of his position. Following the precedent set by Thiers in the case of the

Duchess of Berry, the government elected to treat the would-be challenger of the regime as beside, if not above, the normal legality; his possible exoneration resulting from a jury trial would have been a source of embarrassment. Louis Bonaparte was shipped to America, but in January 1837 a question arose in the Chamber that gave Thiers some concern. It had to do with the precise activity, and the responsibility therefor, of a French agent in Switzerland. Thiers, a minister when this had occurred, was saved by the reluctant willingness of the Chamber to accept the argument of *raison d'état* and the consequent need for secrecy in certain operations.

The net effect of the ministry's coloration and management, its lack of strong personalities and direction, was to bring back together again the two tendencies, left center and right center as they would now be described, the parties of movement and of resistance, of which Thiers and Guizot were the respective leaders; the former's rightward drift was for the moment arrested while Guizot was also discontented. And it was in fact the combination of these two tendencies that resulted in an electoral defeat for the government, following which the Molé ministry resigned in March 1839.

The lack of clear direction was equally manifest in the domain of foreign policy. The Belgian question was finally resolved with the acceptance of the proposed arrangements by the Dutch king and the guarantee by the powers of the perpetual neutrality of Belgium (1839). The last French troops withdrew from Ancona, but on the other side of the Atlantic a more aggressive French policy was pursued with the blockade of Buenos Aires and the occupation of Vera Cruz, both in connection with economic disputes. The assertion on the two sides of the Channel, by Palmerston and Molé respectively, that the community of interests persisted was somewhat less than convincing and was not repeated on the English side in the speech from the throne at the end of 1838.

An easily-put-down rising in Paris in May 1839 bespoke the weariness of the regime, considerable passivity in the country, yet also the persistence of radical ferment. Molé gave way to Soult. The new administration led by Soult was organized as the result of the king playing with skill upon the differences among the leaders of the opposition—Guizot, Thiers, and Odilon Barrot. His success was short-lived, for in February of the following year the Soult ministry was overthrown by an unfavorable vote in the Chamber.

The issue over which it fell was a small enough matter. Following the marriage of one of Louis Philippe's sons, the Duc de Nemours, with a princess of Saxe-Coburg-Gotha, a bill was introduced for the endowment of the couple. To the accompaniment of some rather sordid comments on the king's private resources and his avidity, Thiers and his followers and momentary allies defeated the proposal without further discussion. It was a way of expressing their disapproval of the ministry. The outcome, as four years ealier, and *faute de mieux* in a sense, was to bring Thiers once more to the prime ministership, where he was soon involved in a major foreign policy crisis, to a point of his own making.

During the interval between his two tenures of the office Thiers, as has been shown, played an active role in parliament and politics. But he also enjoyed a measure of leisure that he used to indulge in other activities. Following his fall from office in 1836 he travelled to Italy.[21] Apart from the prestige of ancient Rome that the normal education of the day was calculated to instill, like many alien visitors he fell under the spell of the land, especially its more outstanding artistic achievements. Sailing from Marseilles to Spezia, he proceeded to a villa he had rented near Florence—his means were ample by this time. Florence enchanted him, and in addition to an active social life and the attempted promotion of marital schemes that would join the reigning house of France with the Napoleonic—ex-king Jerome was living in Tuscan exile and had a daughter—he conceived the project of writing a history of Florence. That project never materialized but for a time Thiers pursued it in earnest.

He returned to Paris in the winter to participate in the activity of the Chamber, and the spring of 1837 found him sojourning in Como whence he continued to advance his marital intrigues as well as his literary labors. The former were destined to fail, for the Duke of Orléans shortly married another German princess, of Mecklemburg-Schwerin, but for the latter he enlisted the assistance of some Italian literary men and scholars who helped him gather a large amount of material.

The above-mentioned confused political situation at the beginning of 1839 absorbed all his attention and energy and he spoke at length in the Chamber. The outcome was not at first the expected one. An election turned against the government and the stopgap Soult ministry was the result. Thiers refused the London embassy, offered to him as a sop and for the purpose of removing him from the

Parisian scene. Guizot, however, accepted the post, in which he was to find himself and play an important role through the crisis that arose during the second Thiers ministry, the course of which we shall now proceed to examine.

### CHAPTER 6

# Thiers' Second Prime Ministership
# March–October 1840

THIERS' return to the prime ministership, especially in the light of the above-cited observation of Louis Philippe to the Prussian ambassador at the close of his first tenure of the office, was significant. For it was a measure of the constraints under which the executive had to function, an issue settled long ago in England, but one with which France was, and for that matter still is, struggling in the attempt to define the line of demarcation between powers. To be sure, in a sense there is no final and permanent answer to the problem of the division of power, as the recent debate in American politics would seem to show.

In any case, it was clear in 1840 that the ministry had been brought down by the action, the intrigues if one will, of the Chamber. Thiers certainly believed in limitations on the royal prerogative, in which respect he consistently preferred the English model, just as he continued to favor the English alliance, even despite some frustrations in the operation of it. His chief associate, or rival, Guizot, was at the moment not a serious factor in domestic calculations, having accepted the ambassadorial post at the Court of St. James.

Save for his consistent adherence to the belief in constitutional rule (the king reigns but does not rule), Thiers had travelled some distance in a conservative direction, though to charge him with inconsistency on that score would be going too far. The meaning of his leadership of the Left was not clear, and he certainly had no program of social reform, no very clear program in matters of domestic policy for that matter, being content to maneuver within the possibilities of political trends.

With some domestic problems he had of course to deal, matters financial, the Bank of France, conversion of the rente. He remained moderately protectionist, as in the case of the sugar beet industry, but also showed some flexibility in acknowledging changes in economic conditions. He had earlier taken a rather sceptical view of the desirability of railway construction, but it was he who in June and July advocated the state guarantee of interest for the building of the line to Orleans. He took an interest in the problem of transportation in general, be it canal construction or the establishment of transatlantic lines of steam navigation, and the measures he supported in these matters were adopted. His argument was that France must not fall behind others in new forms of economic activity, but he also stressed the special nature of French trade, luxury goods in considerable measure.

It was the same approach that caused him to favor the expansion of the Algerian establishment, in which he saw a source of future strength. In the context of nineteenth-century imperial activity this was undoubtedly a forward-looking position. As he put it in May:

I say that there is taking place today in the world something that . . . I believe fruitful for the future of mankind, and as for myself I am delighted that my country should have her share in it. For twenty-five years, instead of dashing against each other, the great nations of Europe have remained at peace. . . . Instead of warring among themselves, the great nations of Europe have carried war among the barbarians. . . . And when you claim that Africa is for us a source of weakness, I myself feel that we are drawing strength from it.[1]

Algeria, imperial affairs in general, were as much, in fact rather more, a foreign than a domestic policy matter, and it is in the domain of foreign policy that Thiers' second tenure of the prime ministership is particularly important. It would be anticipating to speak at this time of a grand design aimed at making the Mediterranean a French lake, the bait that Bismarck would dangle before Napoleon III a quarter of a century later. Nevertheless, the Mediterranean was a place of great interest to both Britain and France, the locale where their traditional imperial rivalry was to come to a focus.

England had raised no objection to the French establishment in Algeria—provided it did not spill over east or west into Tunisia or Morocco respectively—and she expected in addition that Algeria would prove to be an entangling diversion for France. As Palmerston put it to Guizot:

You have the regency of Algiers; between you and your Egyptian ally what would be left? Almost nothing, only those poor states of Tunis and Tripoli. The whole African coast and part of the Asiatic coast on the Mediterranean, from Morocco to the Gulf of Alexandretta, would thus be in your power and under your influence. This we cannot accept.[2]

In addition, Palmerston chose to deliver himself of some very harsh comments about French methods of colonization.[3]

### I   The Confrontation with England: Thiers versus Palmerston

But at the eastern end of the Mediterranean the French interest was well established and of long standing. Without reaching back to the Frankish Crusades, more recently that interest had come to focus on Egypt, especially since the Napoleonic adventure in that Turkish province. The looseness of control in the peripheral regions of the Ottoman Empire was what had made possible the rise in Egypt of a virtually independent power. Albanian Mohammed Ali, a soldier in the Turkish service, having got rid of the Mamelukes, had established himself in control. In ruling the country he combined an oriental despotism with an intelligent understanding of the ways of the modern world, which made him the founder of modern Egypt. He directed his energies to the development of the economy and the creation of effective armed power, making use of foreign technical competence, largely in the form of French advisors—de Lesseps, first as consul, later of Suez Canal fame, is a good illustration. As a consequence, Egypt became the chief focus of France's Near Eastern interest.

We saw Mohammed Ali firmly established in Egypt in 1833 as a result of successful war against the Sultan, but his larger ambition had been frustrated by Russian diplomatic intervention. That occasion had been an instance of Anglo-French cooperation in resisting Russian expansionist designs.[4] The defeat rankled with Sultan Mahmoud who prepared for revenge by attempting a reorganization of the Turkish military establishment. It was he who, in 1839, took the initiative of hostilities, the results of which were again disastrous. For in Syria the Egyptians were able to repeat their earlier performance, their position enhanced by the fact that the Turkish fleet, dispatched to Alexandria, went over to their side. The death of Sultan Mahmoud at this juncture, to be succeeded by a youth of sixteen, made the Turkish situation seem altogether hopeless and raised the question of outside intervention: the fate of the Sick Man of Europe was well established as one of the major problems of European diplomacy. Russian intervention seemed the most likely, on the basis of the treaty of 1833; also, as on that earlier occasion, a convergence of the British and French positions might have been expected, but things went otherwise.

The Russians successfully countered that possibility by making approaches to the British with a view to dividing the Anglo-French combination. At the end of 1839 Baron Brunnow in London was able to establish an Anglo-Russian front on the basis of a joint agreement for closure of the Straits. That is where matters stood when Thiers assumed once more the prime ministership in France. Though Thiers, as pointed out, had been a consistent advocate of Anglo-French understanding, he was also a highly nationalistic Frenchman. His counterpart in this instance was not so much Viscount Melbourne, the rather accommodating prime minister, as the foreign minister, Palmerston, an equally nationalistic Englishman, who directed foreign policy, even in the face of some cabinet opposition. Thus the Near Eastern crisis of 1840 came to be in large measure a confrontation between Palmerston and Thiers.

Guizot had been appointed to the French embassy in London in October 1839; he, too, was an accommodating man, one whose interest in and knowledge of things British made him welcome in the British milieu. But Guizot found himself caught between two fires. An involved story may be summed up by saying that Thiers miscalculated. The burden of his policy consisted in procuring a direct agreement between the Porte and its vassal, an arrangement that could then be presented to Europe as a *fait accompli*. On his side, Mohammed Ali also miscalculated, counting on greater French support than was eventually forthcoming.

The stalemate between a seemingly irresistible force and an apparently immovable obstacle was broken by a *coup de théâtre* of Palmerston's contrivance, an effective calling of Thiers' bluff, that his stance of intransigence essentially had been. The news of the quadripartite agreement, including all the powers but France, that was signed in London on July 15, 1840, for a settlement of the Near Eastern problem radically altered the nature of the conflict.

While Britain could agree with France in opposing Russian expansion, she also wanted to preserve the integrity of the Ottoman Empire, an aim to which Palmerston suspected that France was less earnestly dedicated; that was the reason for the determinedly anti-French position he assumed. His suspicions were not wholly devoid of foundation. In January 1840, speaking on the reply to the address from the throne, Thiers had advocated the integrity of the Empire "within the limits of its effective control," clearly a qualified integrity, especially as Thiers also favored extending Mohammed Ali's control to Syria on a hereditary basis; through him, France's protégé, French influence threatened an extension in the Near East that was unacceptable to British purposes.

In that same speech, before taking office, Thiers could be critical of the ambiguity of French policy, but a measure of his misjudgment appears in his own rather grandiloquent language on that occasion:

> Of one thing I am certain, gentlemen: Russia and England may reach a momentary agreement, but the real rivalries will appear one day; then the rivalries will become redoubtable enmities and then our friendship will be sought; everyone will want it; and in order to secure the powerful sword of France, no price will be too great to put before her feet.
>
> I should regret to see France isolated. But I am certain that, even isolated, she could patiently wait for the unfolding of world events.[5]

As late as April he was still speaking in favor of the English alliance.[6] Later still in the year, when the Chamber reassembled, in the course of the debate on the address from the throne, in a very long speech Thiers defended his policy, surveying the whole record with the support of citations from diplomatic correspondence.[7]

When the bombshell of the London Treaty had exploded in July, he was himself in charge of the conduct of French affairs, being both prime and foreign minister. The reaction to the London treaty was very strong in France, not least at the level of opinion, which read it as a resurrection of the anti-Napoleonic coalition, with the consequence that the prospect of war shifted from Syria to the Rhine. The German *Wacht am Rhein* dates from this period while on the French side Musset and Lamartine grandiloquently recalled in their verses the earlier successful French crossings of that river. But it was also shadow boxing. The image of Napoleonic accomplishments in overrunning Europe was after all a distortion, in part due to special circumstances, and Guizot took a more sober and accurate view of the measure of French power. As he put it:

Should France go to war in order that the Pasha of Egypt might keep Syria?

Obviously, this is not a sufficiently large interest to become a cause of war. France, which did not go to war to liberate Poland from Russia and Italy from Austria, cannot reasonably do so in order that Syria should be in the hands of the Pasha rather than of the Sultan.

The war would be either oriental and naval, or continental and general. If naval, the disparity of forces, damages and risks is undeniable. If continental and general, France could only sustain it by giving it a revolutionary character, that is, by abandoning the honest, wise and useful policy which she has followed since 1830, thus herself transforming the alliance of the four powers into a European coalition.[8]

There will be occasion to mention again Guizot's conservative orientation, his leaning toward the eastern powers. Thiers, too, would come to lean increasingly in that direction, for reasons of domestic policy in the main, but at the moment the two differed on the tactics to be used in the specific situation, where Thiers believed in operating from a position of strength. His summation of the significance of his dimissal can be found in the closing remarks of a speech he made in November:

If it [my country] only wishes to save its own territory, there is perhaps no danger in the behavior it has adopted; but if it claims to have a say in the great affairs of Europe, by behaving in the manner that it has it must renounce that hope for a long time.[9]

By this Thiers meant that the price of surrender would be diminished influence, a sound enough judgment. He himself, in July, had not been in favor of surrender. Whether he was still bluffing or willing to face the ultimate consequences of an uncompromising stance, it is the latter impression he conveyed. The armed forces, military and naval, were enlarged and plans were made for the strengthening and modernizing of the fortifications of Paris.

Thiers' conviction that there was no risk in asserting a position of strength resulted in a divergence between himself and the king. In the face of his insistence that France should refuse to accept the Treaty of London while announcing increases in her military establishment, the king balked and flatly refused to accept that advice. Once more, as four years earlier, Thiers' brief tenure of the prime ministership came to an end, his resignation being the clear signal that France would entertain the possibility of compromise.

The end of the story may be briefly indicated, though, his policy having been rejected, Thiers played no part in the final outcome. Where Palmerston was concerned, the tendency was to press the English advantage. However, even in the English cabinet there was opposition to his aggressiveness, and the other European powers showed no desire for an ultimate confrontation.

In the Near East, England had her way. Mohammed Ali, left to his own means without French support and faced with determined British naval action, had no choice but to yield. Confronted with an ultimatum, his larger ambitions, in Syria and beyond, had to be altogether abandoned and he was left in possession of Egypt alone; less than that would have been a setback that even Louis Philippe could not have accepted. That arrangement was ostensibly contrived through a direct agreement between the Pasha and the Sultan, while ostensibly also France rejoined the concert of the powers through her participation in the signature of a convention that dealt with the status of the Straits.

The episode inserts itself to perfection in the long record of Anglo-French imperial rivalry, particularly in the Near East. Once more France had been defeated by England, for the usual reason: that her power was insufficient to deal at the same time with a naval and a land confrontation. Thiers had unquestionably misjudged, though it would be incorrect to see in this instance an illustration of either unreasonable nationalistic intransigence or a determined anti-British position on his part.

*The Return of Napoleon's Remains.*

The departure of Thiers from office may fairly be said to have inaugurated a new phase of the July Monarchy, one that was to last to its end and in which he himself would turn into a leader of the opposition to a course of which Guizot was the main guiding hand. But before tracing Thiers' activity during this period another incident must be mentioned in which he played a major role.

In his *History of the French Revolution,* the period of the Directory in particular, Thiers' admiration of Napoleon is evident, an admiration not diminished by the passing of time, even if he was not blind to the excesses that had led to the downfall of the imperial regime. In 1839 he had committed himself to write a history of the

Consulate and the Empire. By that time the Napoleonic legend was in full bloom in France.

The story about to be related has in it some elements of high comedy. The initiative of returning Napoleon's remains to France seems to have been of English origin, an attempt by Palmerston to create a diversion from the Near Eastern imbroglio as well as to shortcircuit certain intrigues of which Louis Napoleon, returned from his American exile and currently living in England, was the center.[10] Thiers jumped at the idea and instructed a somewhat surprised and less than enthusiastic Guizot—the emperor was not his favorite hero—to approach Palmerston. Feigning surprise in turn, the latter was amenable, and the project moved toward realization once Thiers had extracted the consent of an understandably reluctant Louis Philippe. Thiers saw in the scheme possibly added popularity for himself, a judgment that seemed justified by the enthusiastic reaction in the country to the announcement of the project. The Chamber appropriated one million francs for the operation, though only after some newspapers had opened a subscription for it, and a like sum had been offered by Joseph Bonaparte. On the annual celebration of the July revolution in 1840 Louis Philippe had to endure the strains of the *Marseillaise*, a seditious anthem at the time.

A further incident that, especially in retrospect, can only be described as an added musical comedy turn, occurred at the beginning of August: Louis Napoleon landed surreptitiously on the French coast with the intention of provoking an uprising in the garrison of Boulogne. The escapade—it was no more than that—collapsed in dismal failure, for the claimant to the Napoleonic succession was immediately apprehended and subsequently tried before the Chamber of Peers. Skillfully defended by none other than Berryer,[11] who used the occasion to embarrass the government, he was sentenced to life imprisonment but soon managed to escape.

Thiers had no cause to be unduly alarmed, all the less as his agents had informed him of the prospective attempt, but the conjunction of it with a high state of nationalistic excitement, the enlargement of the armed forces, the plans for the fortification of Paris, a virulent press on both sides of the Rhine—all together had produced an atmosphere of intense and dangerous crisis.

Yet to a point it was also play acting, for no one really wanted war. Nevertheless, the need of cooling tempers was what produced the dissension between Louis Philippe and Thiers and the latter's dismissal in October. When Napoleon's remains finally arrived in Paris, an adequate display of ceremonial pomp was offered to the Parisian populace, a million of whom, on the 15th of December, witnessed the solemn procession through the Arc de Triomphe, down the Champs Élysées, across the Seine over the Concorde bridge, to its ultimate resting place in the Invalides. But it was Soult, the new Prime Minister, and Guizot who presided over the ceremony of which Thiers had been the chief architect.

CHAPTER 7

# Into Opposition Again

## I  *The Advent of Guizot*

THE liquidation of the Near Eastern crisis and the reintegration of France into the European Concert were, appropriately, in considerable measure the work of the French ambassador in London, François Guizot, who had proved a sounder judge than Thiers on this occasion and whose realistic appraisal of the limitations of French power has been mentioned. He was recalled from London to succeed Thiers at the foreign office. Beyond this, for the remainder of the life of the July Monarchy, until 1848, Guizot was in effect the controlling and directing hand of the policy of the regime, both domestically and vis-à-vis the outside. Increasingly during that period his opponent was Thiers, and for that reason a word must be said of Guizot, the chief representative of an opposite, more conservative, tendency.

Ten years Thiers' senior, Guizot also came from the south, having been born in Nîmes. But in terms of personality and disposition the two men stood poles apart. For one thing, Guizot came from a Protestant milieu, and Calvinistic sternness was a marked trait of his character, that a six-year sojourn in Geneva had been calculated to confirm. Though his father was guillotined during the Convention, Guizot did not turn against the initial, more moderate aspects of the Revolution, one point of contact with Thiers. Both men had welcomed the Restoration and during the 1820s had thus been able to collaborate in their support of constitutionalism.

Other points of contact and resemblance: both men were interested in history, in which domain Guizot did rather better work than Thiers, professing the discipline for a time at the University of Paris. Also, though in part for different reasons, both took a strong interest in things English and admired English political institutions.

But Guizot delved farther back than Thiers into the past, dealing with the origins of France, more broadly with those of civilization. The great work of the English historian, Edward Gibbon, attracted his attention, for a critical edition of which he was responsible.

Guizot was fond of the *juste milieu*, the golden mean, an outlook on which Thiers could also agree, since in politics both were convinced believers in the rightness of rule by the qualified competent, those endowed with the sense of responsibility that the possession of property provides, the bourgeois. But the word *juste* is susceptible of flexible interpretation, and the contrast between Calvinistic austerity and the exuberant enjoyment of the goods of the earth is significant. With the passing of time, and especially after he was in office, Guizot became increasingly conservative; in the domain of foreign policy this meant a tendency to draw closer to Metternichian Europe, a tendency that became one important point of divergence with Thiers.

The dismissal of Thiers signalled the inauguration of a new phase of the July Monarchy, one that was to last to the end and in which he himself would turn into a leader of the opposition to a course of which Guizot was the main guiding hand. It is with the activity of Thiers, as leader of that opposition, that we are mainly concerned.

## II  *The Growing Divergence between Thiers and Guizot*

The new ministry was not expected to be lasting, Guizot's own following being neither solid nor large, while he also lacked a strong backing from the king. The differences between Guizot and Thiers, if temperamentally considerable, were not yet overwhelming in political terms, and in 1840 the two men did not seem destined to emerge as the embodiments and the leaders of contrasting tendencies.

The Chamber, which had been in recess since July 15, the very date of the Treaty of London, resumed its sessions in November. The debate on the reply to the speech from the throne naturally turned in considerable measure into one over the Near Eastern events, the high point of the crisis having passed though it was not yet fully resolved. Thiers spoke at length on the 25th and the 27th, giving an account of his handling of the episode, understandably a defense of his actions. Guizot, too, presented his version, claiming, interestingly in the light of his subsequent orientation, that he had been in accord with the government—meaning Thiers—until he perceived the possibility of armed conflict induced by the revolutionary spirit of France.

Yet the debate, while a confrontation between the two men and their policies, was devoid of acerbity. When appropriations for military preparations, the fortification of Paris, came under discussion at the close of the year, Thiers consistently defended their need, in this case helping to save the day for the government.

Thiers' position on a subject of equal significance for the development of the economy and for defense is worth noting. In May 1842 the Chamber debated a governmental project for the construction of a railway network centered on Paris, the scheme that France would eventually realize.[1] Thiers seems to have had an aversion to railways. While admitting the greater progress of other nations in the development of this new mode of transportation, he continued to minimize its usefulness in France, contending that the importance of the German accomplishment in that domain had been exaggerated. Stressing financial soundness, he favored the construction of a single line, a connection between the Channel and the Mediterranean, Lille to Marseilles. That proposal was defeated, and France remained comparatively backward in railway construction, by comparison with Germany in particular, with consequences that would appear thirty years later. Railway construction incidentally proved to be a marvelous field for all sorts of speculation, yet Thiers' conservative insistence on financial soundness must in this particular activity be put down as another case of misjudgment.

At the same time it was also clear that the gap between Thiers and the ministry—Guizot—was widening, even though points of agreement still remained; not on the Near Eastern question to be sure, on the score of which Thiers persisted in defending the course he had adopted and his interpretation of the unfolding of events. Speaking before the Chamber in January 1842, a postmortem performance since the crisis was past and the arrangements for the Near East had been settled, in a long speech[2] he gave an interesting survey of the whole European situation over a long period of time. The dependable opposition of the Germanic powers he saw rooted in their fear of the ideology of which France was the representative, in combination with a persistent suspicion of the French hope of achieving the frontier of the Rhine. England, according to Thiers, was a more variable factor, easier to collaborate with when under a Whig administration. Metternich had skillfully driven a wedge between England and France by espousing the English position in the Near East where Austria herself had no direct interest.

But Thiers continued to maintain that France should have adhered to his policy of negotiating from a position of strength and not allowed herself to be intimidated. The Convention of the Straits, which had been the instrument of France's reintegration into the Concert of Europe, he looked upon with scorn as a meaningless agreement.

There was validity in some of his strictures. The final outcome of the confrontation had undoubtedly been an English success, vis-à-vis France as well as Russia, for the latter country had tacitly abandoned the privileged position obtained by her in the treaty of 1833. The fact remains nevertheless that Thiers' defense was specious and that in Palmerston he had found more than his match: his contention that strength should ever be in the background of negotiations had backfired; that was precisely what Palmerston had done, and in the reckoning the French surrender had been the result of his correct appraisal of the relationship of forces and of the limited possibilities of the French, while in the process Thiers had only managed to convey an impression of obstreperous aggressiveness.

Consistently, however, Thiers continued to object to what he regarded as unnecessary French concessions to England in the right of naval visitation in connection with the current attempt to deal with the slave trade.[3] That question was one of those broached on the occasion of the visit of Queen Victoria to Louis Philippe at Eu in September 1843. That occasion went well, the Queen being highly pleased with the festivities and the graciousness of her host, while Aberdeen, the British foreign secretary, and Guizot found each other congenial. Thiers took a jaundiced view of the whole performance of which he had not been in favor.

*The Spanish Marriages; the end of the Entente*

Queen Victoria's visit to Eu was interpreted in some quarters as indicative of a revival of the Anglo-French Entente Cordiale of the 1830s; the fragility of that connection was about to be exposed again. That the breach occurred over an issue of very minor importance only emphasized that the tradition of rivalry between the two countries was still the dominant aspect of their relations.

The so-called Quadruple Alliance of 1834, consisting of Britain, France, and the liberal elements in the two states of the Iberian peninsula, following the common position adopted by the governments on both sides of the Channel, fitted Thiers' view of the desirability of their cooperation. He drew a picture of the decline of French fortunes following the parting of their ways,[4] for all that he himself had presided over the break and could be charged with a measure of responsibility for it. He ought to have taken greater heed of Palmerston's above-cited concern about the too-great extension of French influence in the Mediterranean.[5] Algeria, the Levant, and Spain constituted in British eyes but different aspects of a whole. The first was becoming French, but the outcome of the Near Eastern crisis had effectively checked French designs in that quarter. It is of interest that, at the same time that Mohammed Ali was being pushed back into Egypt, British stock in Madrid, under the Esparto ministry, was rising at the expense of the French. Commercial rivalry, though it existed, took second place to political considerations.

The coming of the second Peel administration in England in September 1841, which was to last five years, seemed to open the possibility of restoring Anglo-French harmony. Aberdeen at the foreign office was a very different man from Palmerston, not least in the style he adopted; the sympathetic understanding between him and his French counterpart, Guizot, has been indicated. The above-mentioned visit of Queen Victoria to Eu was the outward manifestation of the restored harmony. Spanish affairs were discussed on that occasion, the problem being that of finding a suitable spouse for the young Spanish queen, declared of age at the tender age of thirteen. Dynastic connections, though of less moment than in the days of the war of the Spanish Succession, still carried a certain weight, and the suitable compromise was the exclusion of both the French candidate, the Duke of Montpensier, son of Louis Philippe, and the British, the prince of Saxe-Coburg, cousin of Victoria's prince consort. There matters rested for a time, while Louis Philippe returned Queen Victoria's visit; she once more came to Eu and meantime other possibilities were considered for the hand of the Spanish queen.

But the fundamental and traditional rivalry between the two countries could not be so easily compromised and it manifested itself in many forms and many quarters. France's protectionist policy, and attempted customs union with Belgium that King Leopold abandoned under British pressure, France's too active expansion in

Algeria threatening to spill over the entire Maghreb, petty disputes in the Pacific,[6] kept alive the reciprocal distrust.

It was in this clouded climate that Guizot thought to score a success. He chose to promote the candidacy of the Duke of Montpensier for the hand of the Spanish queen's sister, Isabella. To the accompaniment of intrigues, in which French and English diplomacy in Madrid sank to levels at once sordid and comical, the issue was apparently resolved with the simultaneous marriage of Montpensier to Isabella and of the Spanish queen to the Duke of Cadiz. As doubts were broadly entertained about the likelihood of issue from this second marriage, the English feeling was that a French prince had secured a position "on the footstool of the Spanish throne."

This seeming French success occurred in September 1846, by which time Palmerston had returned to the foreign office, not the man to take such doings lying down. Amid charges and countercharges of double dealing, and while Queen Victoria shared Palmerston's indignation at the French king's supposed duplicity, the premature Entente Cordiale came to an end.

Thiers had occasion to comment on the changed nature of the alliance, even before the dissension over Spanish affairs. He attributed it in considerable measure to the return of the Tories to power, and made the valid point that the very grounds of agreement, over Belgium and Spain for example, political issues in the main, had served to shift the emphasis to the commercial ones, on which differences prevailed. The question of which country had undergone the greater change may be left open, but certainly Thiers' tune had altered. As he put it, in reference to the Eastern Question:

It is undoubtedly in the Orient that the most serious, the most embarrassing contrasts, will have their roots. It is true that the two giants, the maritime and the continental, in dispute over the most beautiful and decisive positions of the globe, will confront each other. That day come, France being free, holding in suspense her formerly so powerful sword, which I hope has not lost its edge in our enfeebled hands, throwing that sword in one of the scales of the balance, will tip it violently and thus decide victory. That day may be distant, but at the moment the mere prospect of such an act by France constitutes an immense moral force.[7]

Yet Thiers persisted in his belief in the need to deal from a position of strength. On other occasions the same year, and at the opening of the new parliamentary session, he was strongly critical of what he attacked as Guizot's policy of always yielding to England, be it in Morocco, Tahiti, or the right of naval visitation in the fight against the slave trade, inducing in the process an occasional sharp exchange with Guizot, as in the course of his long and vigorous speech on May 29.

### III  *Leader of the Opposition*

History books picture Thiers as leader of the opposition to the government during the decade of the 1840s. Such an image is not incorrect, though it must be set in the proper context of the tone of the political life of the country during that period. The fundamental grounds of Thiers' opposition were well put in his own words on the occasion of the debate on the speech from the throne in January 1846. Speaking on the 20th, he put it thus:

> It is true that in my opinion (and I may be mistaken) the monarchy is not understood and practiced today as I should wish that it should be and as I believe that it ought to be. It is true that in my view it should be closer to what it is in England, where, I believe, the only type of monarchy acceptable to a great and enlightened nation is practiced. With such views and feelings it was impossible for me to remain long in the government. I joined the opposition; however, in joining that opposition I continued to adhere to the belief in constitutional monarchy, but monarchy in any case. . . .
>
> Since 1830 I believed that peace was the most desirable condition for our government. . . . But I believed that it could be obtained in surer and more dignified conditions. I may have been mistaken, but however that may be, that is the second reason for my joining the opposition. [8]

In other words, Thiers was in disagreement with the government on both domestic and foreign policy. But his opposition was not doctrinaire and virulent, leaving room for agreement on certain points. Thus, following the accidental death of the Duke of Orléans, Thiers supported the arrangement proposed by the government in regard to a regency, a support for which Guizot expressed thankfulness.

The election of July 1842 had gone in the government's favor and Thiers was relatively inactive in parliamentary debates. He could put time on his *History of the Consulate and the Empire*, the first volume of which appeared in 1845 and on which more will have to be said.

The first half of the decade was generally a low point in political activity. It was also a time of fair economic prosperity, the high point of the period best summarized in Guizot's advice, *enrichissez-vous*. With the franchise restricted as it was, the differences of views among the narrow ruling bourgeois class remained confined to very restricted dimensions, the accent being rather on a large measure of consensus. The workers, the great mass of the French people, had no voice in their government, and it would be a misunderstanding to equate the tendencies and factions of the day with the organized political parties, in France and elsewhere, of a later time.

That shrewd observer, de Tocqueville, gave apt expression to the uninspiring lack of diversity. As he wrote, "I have spent ten years of my life in the company of very great minds which agitated themselves without being capable of deep involvement, and which used all their perspicacity in looking for subjects of substantial difference without being able to discover any"; and again, "in control of everything to a degree that no aristocracy had ever been or will be capable of achieving, the middle class, become the government, became identified with private industry. . . . Posterity will perhaps never know the extent to which the government of this time had toward the end taken on the appearance of an industrial enterprise in which the guiding inspiration is the achieving of the profits that the shareholders can derive from it."[9]

Guizot's facile answer—"progress is promised by all political parties, a conservative policy will alone give it to you"—found its counterpart in the famous rejoinder, *la France s'ennuie*.

## The Problem of Education

Ferment there was, nevertheless, that would eventually bear fruit. To cite but some random examples: Auguste Comte's *Cours de Philosophie Positive* appeared between 1830 and 1842, to be followed by his *Système de Philosophie Positive* (1846–1854); de Tocqueville, whose *Democracy in America* appeared during the second half of the 1830s, was a member of parliament; and 1840 was the year when Proudhon's famous *What is Property?* was presented to the public. The issue of relations between church and state, a perennial in France, centering particularly on the control of education, was one on which largely Voltairean bourgeois and more traditional aristocrats could join battle; the issue was an important subject of debate in the otherwise quiet and dull atmosphere of the 1840s.

The whole French system of education had been molded by Napoleon, though the influence of the *ancien régime* remained strong, and the reforms introduced by the Revolution, the Convention especially, had been integrated into the new arrangements. The central issue remained the extent of control and supervision that the state should exercise over private institutions, in other words the granting of teaching licenses and of degrees. Private instruction essentially meant that given by Catholic institutions. In 1833, Guizot, minister of education at the time, had been responsible for the introduction of legislation that was then regarded as liberal. But since that time what might be called a Catholic offensive had quietly been under way, which tended to equate freedom in education with a minimum of state interference. For one thing the Jesuits had unobtrusively returned, and to their activity the state had on the whole turned a blind eye.

The debate sharpened in the 1840s, much of it centering on what was called the monopoly of education. Monopoly of control in the hands of the state was regarded by Catholics as an infringement upon their liberty, while, conversely, their opponents felt that a conservative Catholic Church took shelter behind the libertarian slogan to establish a monopoly of its own, hence constituted in turn a threat to liberty. In parliament the debate came to focus on the legislation introduced in 1841 by Villemain, the minister of education. The issue remained dormant until discussion of it was resumed in 1844. Meanwhile, the work of Michelet and Quinet, *Des Jésuites*, the outcome of their lectures at the Collège de France, in 1844 created quite a stir. With the growing strength of the national state, especially such a centralized one as the French, the old problem of the citizen's first allegiance was central; Catholicism in general, the Jesuits in particular, represented possible first allegiance to an outside power, the Roman Pope in this instance.

Thiers was rapporteur of the commission that had examined the governmental scheme and in that capacity delivered a very long speech in the Chamber, on July 13, 1844, explaining and defending the gist of the report. It is an interesting speech, equally revealing of the state of the controversy in France at the time and of Thiers' own orientation in general.

His view of the proper social structure, the central role of the
bourgeoisie, was clearly acknowledged in the crucial place he gave
to secondary education:

> Secondary education molds what are called the enlightened classes of a
> nation. And if the enlightened classes are not the whole nation, they give it
> its character. Their vices, their qualities, their inclinations, good or bad,
> soon become those of the whole nation; they shape the people itself through
> the contagion of their ideas and their feelings.

Stressing the different meaning of freedom in the domain of education from that in the commercial, he emphasized the importance of
the rights and the role of the twin authorities, the father (the family)
and the state; then, following a survey of the course of education in
France, he went on to assert that the ultimate supervisory role
belonged to the University,[10] meaning the state, even though the
Church should not be deprived of the right to provide instruction.

Incidentally, and although it is a side issue, but one also important in our day, his description of the proper content of the curriculum is worth noting for its modern touch. The stress was on the
study of the past and on philosophy, this last a typical French requirement, and Thiers complained that too much information was
demanded of the student. He returned to the charge in a speech in
May of the following year, insisting on the application of the law to
the Jesuits.[11]

# CHAPTER 8

# *The Unmaking of a King*

## I   *Thiers' Criticism of the Regime*

THE drab regime, under Guizot's continuing guidance, was wearing down, and the opposition to it among the *pays légal*, the minute section of those entitled to a say in the conduct of the country's affairs, was continuing to perform in a manner that reminds one of shadow boxing. Thiers' own opposition was mainly based on two grounds, his objection to personal power and his criticism of the conduct of foreign affairs.

In the closing days of the life of the Chamber issued from the elections of 1842, a consultation that had gone in the government's favor, the budget of the interior was discussed in May 1847. This was an important occasion, for it turned in considerable measure into a debate between the two main leaders of the contrasting tendencies. The very long and eloquent speech of which Thiers delivered himself on the 27th amounted to a broad reassertion of principle in the form of reviewing the course of the July Monarchy so far.

According to him, as frequently happened, the regime had evolved from defending the right to espousing the wrong. The initial combination of moderation with firmness had worked well, reestablishing internal order and maintaining the peace abroad. But, once it had felt securely established, the regime had yielded to the flattering approbation of the conservative states of Europe and mistakenly parted company with kindred liberal England. This new orientation did not matter very much where impotent Spain was concerned, but powerful England had been resentful and effectively sought revenge.

That was the key to her successful opposition, in the Near East for example. And the subsequent attempts to renew the connection with England by courting her with unwise concessions (the right of

85

naval visitation, the Pritchard affair) had merely conveyed an impression of weakness and proved unrewarding; her opposition had persisted, in Greece and Syria for example, and been accentuated by the clumsy French handling of the affair of the Spanish marriages.

The persistence in that foreign policy orientation was but another facet of the domestic tendency of the government, which had increasingly become narrowly partisan, as shown by such things as the pressure for the election of "official" candidates, the efforts to control and subvert the press, as well as the position taken on the subject of education. To cap it all, the armed services, despite army increases and the fortification of Paris, the navy in particular, had been neglected, and financial management had had recourse to excessive borrowing.

Guizot and the minister of the interior—the Prime Minister, Soult, mattered little—replied to Thiers' strictures and their reply was followed by a brief rejoinder on the 29th, in the course of which Thiers uttered this caution:

> However, preserve me from making sinister forecasts! Oh, no! I have faith in the country, I have faith in the strength of its institutions, I believe that France will in future correct, through the electoral process alone, that which sixteen years ago she had to correct through a revolution.

The tableau sketched by Thiers of the course of the regime and its deviant orientation was not devoid of speciousness and it was also to a point an argument *pro domo*—who after all had been in charge at the height of the 1840 confrontation with England? Nevertheless, there was also point to his accusations, and it could hardly be denied that Guizot seemed increasingly attracted to the model of Metternichian Europe.[1]

## II  *Switzerland and Italy*

But Guizot would not deviate from his course. Two distinct, but not unrelated, events affected the whole European situation during the second half of the 1840s. An economic crisis was one, poor crops in 1846 and a general lowering of industrial activity creating unemployment and a climate conducive to social and political unrest in contrast with the prosperity that had prevailed during the preceding years. In France nothing comparable to the Irish potato famine occurred, but France was also affected and, unlike Ireland, she contained a reservoir of industrial workers long familiar with political agitation, who in addition felt cheated by the outcome of the 1830 revolution. Metternich was aware of the discontent that was abroad in Europe; as he put it in 1847, "The world is very ill, and the sickness is spreading every day." The other source of concern lay in two areas, adjacent to his own domain, that especially attracted his attention; they were Italy and Switzerland.

In the latter federation, operating under the 1815 constitution, the formation of a conservative league of seven Catholic cantons, the *Sonderbund*, organized as early as 1845, led to a resolution in the federal Diet that demanded the dissolution of the *Sonderbund*. The result was civil war in 1847, a contest between liberal and conservative forces along lines of religious division. The former were successful and proceeded to draft a new constitution that was proclaimed in 1848.

The reason for mentioning this episode is that in the situation, instead of France supporting the liberal elements, Guizot rather aligned himself with Metternich; while not daring to go so far as to advocate intervention, he made no secret of his conservative sympathies. That there was no outside intervention in favor of the Catholic cantons was rather the result of Palmerston's restraining opposition to it, which had the effect of containing the contest within the purely Swiss milieu.

In Italy, Pope Gregory XVI, who died in 1846, was succeeded by Pius IX who inaugurated his reign with certain liberal enactments. These elicited considerable response in the whole peninsula where liberal forces took heart from the Roman development. In Italy, as elsewhere in Europe at the time, these elements tended to look to Paris rather than to Rome for leadership and support.

In all of Italy Austria was the paramount power and Metternich was ready to furnish assistance in the suppression of liberal agitation, which he did in his own domain of direct control, in Milan and in adjacent northern states, while in the south the Neapolitan king earned the epithet of King Bomba for his bombardment of Palermo in subduing the local insurrection in January 1848.

It was in that month that the recessed French Chamber resumed its sessions and proceeded to discuss matters both domestic and foreign. On the 25th Thiers delivered a long speech, in the main an attack on the financial management of the regime, repeating his criticisms of the preceding May.

A few days later, on January 31, and again on May 2, he addressed himself in the main to the Italian and Swiss situations, on which his criticisms were no less virulent. With respect to the former he made the cogent observation that the respect of treaties was a two-way affair; if France ought not to interfere in Italy, neither should Austria. But for the rest liberal movements should find a sympathetic response in France, and he would address the peoples of Italy as follows:

> Let all the populations stretching from Turin to Florence, to Naples, to Palermo, join into a whole, and let them face the common enemy, with at their head Pius IX holding the keys of St. Peter in his hand, and Charles Albert with the ancient sword of the Dukes of Savoy! Rest assured that in that position you would command respect. But should it be otherwise, should attempts be made against your rights and your independence, you may have the assurance that the heart of France is not frozen!

And more than this:

> France and England could perhaps speak jointly; forgetting dissensions not rooted in national interests, they would utter not only the language of treaties, but that of humanity and liberty![2]

Coming from a man experienced in the operation of politics, hence little open to the charge of naïveté, this flight of oratory is of special interest and may be set against the language he would use twenty years later in the face of the accomplished unity of Italy and the impending one of Germany.[3]

As to Switzerland, as he put it in reply to Guizot's own reply to his speech of February 2, "I do not want to create in Switzerland a fragment of the Holy Alliance, in connivance with M. de Metternich."[4] And he also delivered himself of what may be read as a declaration of faith,

> I am not a radical, as radicals well know. . . . But understand clearly my position. I belong to the party of Revolution, in France as well as in Europe; I wish the government of the Revolution to remain in the hands of moderate men. I shall do all I can to insure that it continues so; but when the government will fall in the hands of men less moderate than myself and my friends, in the hands of ardent men, be they radicals, I shall not abandon my cause for that reason; I shall always be of the party of the Revolution.[5]

Thiers was indeed no radical and what he meant by the party of the Revolution was clear; of the consistency of his views his record so far is conclusive evidence.

### III  *The End of the July Monarchy*

The weariness of the worn-down regime was apparent, that the Prussian ambassador judged with accuracy, reporting to his government on February 13, "It may be over tomorrow, just as it may last a little longer. . . . All that can be said is that the machinery put together in 1830 has lost all vitality."[6] Yet Louis Philippe had not given up; despite Guizot's reluctance to withdraw, he thought that some concessions and a ministerial rearrangement might suffice to save the situation.

The pressure had been mounting from a variety of quarters for the departure of the increasingly unpopular minister. One of its manifestations had taken the form of banquets, gatherings of protest that had been initiated as early as the middle of the preceding year. The focus of the agitation was a demand for reform, both electoral—an enlargement of the electorate through a lowering of the property qualification—and parliamentary—restrictions on the eligibility of holders of governmental office.

One banquet, that turned out to be the final catalytic agent, had been scheduled in Paris for January 19.[7] It was banned and postponed, its promoters undecided on the desirability of forcing the issue. Bearing in mind Thiers' own distrust of the mob, his insistence on the rule of the highly financially qualified, it is not surprising to find him opposed to the occasion, which he feared might lead to an ugly confrontation. But a large gathering of people called by the sponsors took place on February 22 in front of the Madeleine. It was the beginning of the end, the transformation of one regime into another, as in 1830, effected in the brief space of three days. The aftermath, however, took longer this time, the effective change to another stability lasting three years.

The indecisive arrangements had the effect of putting tempers on edge. By the evening of the 22nd there was much restlessness in the center of Paris; but the king still hoped to be able to control the situation, though the cries of *A bas Guizot!* raised by the National Guard began to shake his confidence. He finally yielded to the extent of dismissing Guizot, still thinking that the crisis could be overcome by forming another ministry to be headed by Molé. It was too late for that sort of patchwork solution; it was clear that Thiers alone might still succeed in saving the day, having become the rallying focus of the opposition to Guizot, the two men become symbols of the antagonistic tendencies.

Thiers was willing, though reluctant, to work with the unpopular Bugeaud, whom the king had put in charge of the armed forces of the city. Because of the inadequate equipment and preparation of these forces, Thiers thought the Tuileries might be unsafe and elaborated a scheme for the withdrawal of the royal family to the safety of St. Cloud, gaining time to organize an adequate military force for the eventual subduing of Paris in case of necessity, a plan that calls to mind the one that he would put into execution twenty years later.[8]

But Thiers, too, had misjudged. The Parisian populace was turning ugly; fickle as the mob can be, cries of *A bas Thiers!* could be heard not long after those of *Vive Thiers! Vive la Réforme!* had resounded. On the night of February 23–24 Louis Philippe went through a performance reminiscent of that through which Charles X had gone eighteen years before, signing his abdication in favor of his small grandson, the Count of Paris.

As on the earlier occasion, that attempt, too, was overtaken by events. Thiers himself had to make way for the more radical Odilon Barrot; the insurrection was unleashed and assuming control. Amid scenes of confusion, the Tuileries, then the Palais Bourbon were invaded, the Duchess of Orléans, prospective regent, fleeing from the Chamber to the Invalides. There had been no resistance on the part of the armed forces. In the tumult of the Chamber, invaded by the mob, Lamartine for a brief moment sought to contain its urge, proposing the setting up of a provisional government. Following the example of the restored monarchy in 1830, the July monarchy dissolved, the royal family also taking the road of English exile.

In the Chamber Thiers, too, had made a brief and ineffectual appearance, after which he had withdrawn. Clearly, he had miscalculated, a victim in a sense of the ambiguity of his own, too narrowly legalistic position; for he had after all been in fundamental agreement with the essential base of the regime, control in the hands of a small propertied class, while content to attack more limited aspects of the system, the extent of personal power of the king and its foreign policy. The France of 1848 could not repeat the performance of 1688 England, and the epithet "glorious" has not become attached to the Parisian performance of the later date.

It was not long before a new regime would arise in France, which for Thiers was to mean a period of eclipse, until he would once more reemerge, first in opposition again, then finally in full control himself. Through these vicissitudes we shall follow him in the second part of this essay.

### CHAPTER 9

# The Second French Republic

## I  The Frustrated Revolution

C LEARLY the first task of the successful revolution was the organization of a new form of government. This was done with expedition, but, in view of the central role of France in the eyes of liberal Europe, the foreign situation could with equal rapidity become a major issue. The news of the Parisian events, as it spread into mid Europe, had immediate and large repercussions: Berlin, Vienna, the whole Germanic world as well as the Italian, were thrown into turmoil that was serious enough to induce Metternich himself to abandon his post. One large question was whether the successful French revolutionaries would offer their assistance to brother liberals abroad, a hope entertained by the latter and correspondingly feared by the challenged establishments.

The answer to the possibility of French intervention was forthcoming very shortly and showed that Metternich's pessimistic appraisal was at least premature. As early as March 4 the foreign minister in the French provisional government, none other than the poet Lamartine, announced that France would not intervene outside her borders. As it eventually turned out, there would be some French intervention, but it remained confined to the Roman locale, and it is therefore fair summation to say that France adhered to nonintervention, thereby giving grounds for the judgment that by her behavior she saved the peace at the cost of killing the revolution.

Something will have to be said of the Roman and other situations, but in view of the French abstention, especially in the initial stages of the 1848 upheaval throughout much of Europe, it will be convenient to focus first on the course of domestic events. Their unfolding very quickly overtook and left behind those who, like Thiers, had

had but a limited quarrel with the government of Louis Philippe, on the fundamental bases of which they, after all, agreed. The driving force of the 1848 revolution was as much the demand for social as for political reform. Two things in particular make this clear: France was proclaimed a republic, the very word full of radical connotations in the context of the day; and, consistently with this radical orientation, the decision was taken to hold the impending elections under the dispensation of universal (manhood) suffrage, a very radical measure indeed and one well calculated to alarm conservative and moderate opinion, certainly that of Thiers.

It was thus fitting that Thiers should have no place in the provisional government, in which such men as the (previously) radical Lamartine now represented the moderate tendency. Thiers nevertheless remained an important figure in the French political landscape. If he considered universal suffrage at once absurd and dangerous, the word *republic* did not a priori frighten him, the more important issue in his view being that of the location of controls in a republican, or in any other, regime. His appraisal is aptly expressed in a letter he wrote to a friend in Aix on March 4, little over a week after the successful revolution:

> I believe that a moderate republic is today the most desirable thing. The men who have taken control of the provisional government are behaving so far in a manner reassuring to sensible [*honnêtes*] people. Their intentions are very good. But, like all France, I am less fearful of what is than of what may be. We are threatened . . . by the workers' communism, which, if not checked, will make impossible all industry and all commerce and will ruin the country. . . .
>
> I am, from morning to night, surrounded by people, overwhelmed by the consideration shown to me by all parties. . . .
>
> I shall do all that my fellow citizens will make it possible for me to do, content if after so many mishaps, and having witnessed so many impotent monarchical essays, I saw at last a wise and impressive Republic governing the country.[1]

Thiers was guilty of some exaggeration. Yet, if there was no place for him in the provisional government, his established position was responsible for his playing an active, though not a controlling, part in the affairs of the Second Republic. It certainly was not his intention to be content with a role of effacement.

The acknowledgment of the right to work and the institution of the National Workshops, an emergency response to dangerously widespread unemployment, as early as February 26, were measures that were anathema to Thiers, though the simultaneous refusal to adopt the red flag bespoke some moderation. The disarrayed elements of the Right were attempting to rally in the face of the radical mood of the workers, who on their side ineffectually demonstrated in March, an occasion on which even Louis Blanc[2] endeavored to exert a moderating influence.

In this uncertain climate the elections in April turned into an overwhelming victory for the moderate republicans, the tendency that Lamartine best represented. The country as a whole was not as radically inclined as the Parisian workers, a condition that would be registered again before much time had passed. Thiers was not a candidate in the consultation, his place in the Aix constituency being taken by the more radical Berryer, who enjoyed the support of Émile Ollivier,[3] the local prefect. This was to him the source of some bitterness, but his popularity was sufficient to insure his being returned in several constituencies in the June by-elections, when he chose to represent the Seine Inférieure.

By this time events were taking a different turn. The whole spring passed in continued uncertainty, the discontent of the Parisian workers venting itself in demonstrations, such as the one in March already mentioned, or the invasion of the Assembly by the mob on May 15, a scene reminiscent of the *journées* of the Convention. The abolition of the National Workshops in June sparked further discontent; granting their inefficient and boondoggling aspect, they had nevertheless provided some relief to a mass of people whose misery was profound.

The conservative forces of order had sufficiently rallied by this time and General Cavaignac, the war minister, was entrusted by the Assembly with virtually dictatorial powers that he used with effective ruthlessness. For three days, June 23–25, Paris was the scene of civil war, the armed forces putting down the workers, a small preview of March 1871. Save for a few isolated instances in the rest of the country, the Parisian insurrection met with little response or support.

Once more, as on earlier and on subsequent occasions, the forces of order were triumphant and the initial thrust of the revolution frustrated. There has been much discussion among historians about the place and significance of the 1848 revolutions, in France and elsewhere in Europe. It would be difficult to contend that in the short term they did not fail of their central purpose of radical social transformation. Yet it is equally true that they amount to an episode, a lost battle, in a long and continuing war, the trend of the contest remaining consistently and inescapably in one direction, a stage in the tortuous record of the mass coming into its own.

In any case, just-reelected Thiers could now take his place and make his influence felt in more congenial surroundings. His participation in legislative proceedings was both active and telling, and it is worth noting that in the parliamentary debates of the next three years he usually received the plaudits of the Right, in contrast with the applause that had been his from the opposition to the July Monarchy; during the June days the cry of *A bas Thiers!* had been heard in the streets of Paris. His position—he was just fifty years of age at this time—had crystallized and a practical man he remained.

### Property Must be Defended

The June rising and its suppression were subjects of debate in the Assembly, where the problem of finances was also under discussion; the course of events since February had contributed to the intensification of the economic and financial crisis that had itself been one of the causes of the revolution. Joseph Proudhon had been elected to the Assembly at the same time as Thiers. Proudhon is generally associated with the libertarian anarchist tendency, his lapidary summation, *la propriété c'est le vol* (property is theft), sufficiently known. Come to Paris in February, he proceeded to publish a newspaper, *Le Représentant du Peuple*, in which he advocated his ideas. His role in 1848 is not of great importance, but his membership in the legislature gave him an opportunity to propose legislation aiming at the implementation of his views, specifically in the matter of taxation and credit.

It fell to Thiers, a member of the finance committee, to report on Proudhon's proposals, expounded at the end of July. In a speech on August 2 Thiers defended his condemnation of the Proudhonian heresy; it is a measure of the temper of the Assembly that Proudhon's proposals were rejected by a vote of 540 to 2, on a resolution that read in part as follows:

Considering that the proposal of citizen Proudhon is an odious attack against the principles of public morality; that it violates property. . . . Considering besides that its author has maligned the revolution of February 1848 by presenting it as an accomplice of the theories he has expounded. . . .[4]

But Thiers did more. He was sufficiently exercised by the pernicious attacks against property that he had used his relative leisure before the election to write a book on the subject. With his wonted facility, in the course of three months he produced a more than 400-page treatise, suitably entitled *De la Propriété*. Not a work of the most profound thought, it evinces nevertheless broad knowledge, drawing upon history, economics, and psychology, and constitutes a considered exposition of a point of view that goes into detailed discussion of the bases of property, the fallacies of communism and socialism as understood at the time, and the proper bases of taxation. Considering the importance of the issue, a few quotations seem appropriate, though space compels us to be brief:

All the advocates of a social revolution in varying degrees attack property. . . . One must therefore combat all these odious, puerile, ridiculous but disastrous systems born like a multitude of insects out of the decomposition of all governments.[5]

Bearing in mind the fundamentals of human nature and the necessities of social organization, "I shall be able to say: property is a right, as legitimately as I say: liberty is a right."[6] And again, society has an interest in guaranteeing the right of property, for "without that guarantee there is no labor, without labor no civilization, . . . but only misery, brigandage and barbarism."[7]

The following has a very contemporary ring: "Society having been oppressed by the dominance of the upper classes until 1789, we are seeing it oppressed from 1848 by the reverse domination."[8] On a more philosophical tone, the heading of the concluding chapter stated

That there exists in society a measure of evil that governments must endeavor to redress, and that there is another element, inherent in human nature, from which men cannot be shielded by any conceivable perfection of government.[9]

The book sold very well. The party of order, or "moral order" as the popular phrase went, could count on an effective spokesman.

## The Constitution of 1848

Meanwhile, with considerable expeditiousness, a project of constitution had been drafted. The various bureaus of the Assembly submitted the results of their deliberations to the constitutional committee of that body, which as a whole discussed the projected new constitution in September and October. The constitution finally proclaimed in November vested sovereignty in the people, who were to exercise their powers through representation, and, interestingly, as in the American case, it instituted the separation of powers.

On two occasions in particular Thiers intervened in the discussion of constitutional matters. On September 13 the issue under consideration was that of the implementation of the right to work, specifically a provision stating that "the Republic must protect the citizen in his person, his family, his religion, his property. It recognizes the right of all citizens to education, assistance and work." Note that this was 1848, not the mid-twentieth century. The right to work, especially, was to Thiers a nefarious innovation, a position in which he had de Tocqueville's support.

Somewhat cavalierly dismissing the Republic ("we have not desired the Republic, we accept it"), he went on to assert the same general views that his book had expounded. Society rested on three principles: property, the product of labor; liberty, an inalienable right; and competition, the source of lower prices and higher salaries for workers. The newfangled ideas were pernicious: communism would encourage slothfulness; association would produce industrial anarchy; reciprocity would lead to price controls and paper money; the right to work, most dangerous of all, meant institutionalizing the payment of the unemployed, who should indeed not be ignored but at most be entitled to some form of assistance. In Thiers' view guaranteeing employment to all would be tantamount to providing an army for the insurrection—remember the National Workshops. Following an intense debate, Thiers' position carried the day.

The other occasion of Thiers' intervening, in October, involved the issue of army recruitment. The constitutional project envisaged universal conscription, excluding the possibility of procuring a substitute, a possibility obviously available to the affluent alone. Universal conscription, too, may be seen as an assertion of the democratic principle, the equal liability of all citizens for defense.

But Thiers argued against that institution, enlarging on the virtues of a professional army, explaining the different conditions that obtained in the British and the Prussian milieus, resorting to a measure of sophistry in the process. In the reckoning, the possibility of substitution, clearly a privilege of the well-to-do, was adopted.[10]

One important issue was that of the mode of choice of the president. That perennial of French politics since the Revolution, the power of the executive, was involved, some advocating the necessity of a strong power at the center, others fearful of the possible abuse of such an arrangement. Thiers took no part in this particular debate, the outcome of which was the decision that the president would be popularly elected instead of by the Assembly, an attempted expression of the belief in the separation of powers.

## II   Enter Louis Napoleon Bonaparte

The discussion of the presidential position was overshadowed and in some respects influenced by the intrusion of the personality of Louis Napoleon, a nephew of the first Napoleon and the carrier of whatever claim—not a very strong claim—there might be to a Napoleonic succession on any basis of legitimacy. This man we have already met in connection with the rather ineffectual attempts to provoke risings among the armed forces, at Strasbourg in 1836, at Boulogne in 1840. This last had resulted in a life sentence of imprisonment, but he had managed to escape and return to his English exile. Banned from France, associated at one point with the Italian *carbonari,* he had spent most of his youth in Germany and Switzerland. His interest in the social question had found expression in a book, *The Extinction of Pauperism,* of mildly socialistic inspiration.

From London Louis Napoleon followed with interest the French events of 1848, but he was wise enough to remain uninvolved in their initial unfolding. After he was elected to the Assembly at a June by-election, his awkwardness had made in that body a very poor impression, that a Germanic accent did little to alleviate. He was not felt to be a threat, and Thiers' judgment—"a fool that it will be possible to lead"—if unusually harsh, also conveyed a hint of future possibilities.

The candidacy of Thiers for the presidential position, as leader of the "party of order," the conservative tendency in the context of the time, was an obvious one. But he preferred to abstain, pretexting that "if I should succeed I should be obliged to marry the Republic, and I am too honest a fellow to marry such a bad girl (*mauvaise fille*)."[11] That, however, did not mean renouncing an important role, albeit one behind the scenes; Thiers was an experienced man in the upsetting and the making of regimes. There were negotiations between Thiers, Louis Napoleon, and Cavaignac, the current holder of the executive office and himself a candidate in the election. The outcome of these somewhat intricate proceedings was Thiers' espousal one week before the balloting of the Napoleonic candidacy, in rather qualified terms: "Though not asserting that the election of Monsieur Louis Bonaparte is a good, it seems to all of us moderate men, a lesser evil."[12]

Thiers had been giving Louis Napoleon advice, the result of which was the announced Napoleonic program, a manifesto issued on November 29; it was an ambiguous appeal to all shades of opinion under the cover of the Napoleonic name, "symbol of order and security," commodities for which the demand was considerable.

The result of the election on December 10 came as a surprise to the leaders of opinion, though it perhaps should not have in view of the conservative tendency that the French electorate as a whole had evinced in the April elections for the Assembly, to which now was added the not inconsiderable appeal of the Napoleonic name. This was only the first instance of the prospective incumbent's practice of the art of meaning all things to all men, a technique that he was soon to master even without Thiers' guiding counsel. The votes of the peasants and the workers, who responded to the appeal, far outnumbered the combined ones of bourgeois and radicals. Louis Napoleon received seventy-five percent of the vote,[13] and he took office on December 20.

It would have been logical for Thiers to enter the government, but if he could not have the first place in it he preferred to continue in the role of *éminence grise*, a role of considerable importance—for a time at least. Thus Odilon Barrot headed the new ministry, which consisted mainly of former supporters of the July Monarchy. Louis Napoleon consistently sought Thiers' advice, though he did not always choose to follow it, as in the case of his personal military establishment, when Thiers had counseled less ostentatious, civilian garb and an American simplicity of outward behavior.

Immediately the question arose of the relationship between the Assembly and the government, the latter anxious to be rid of the control of the former. In January 1849 there was an alarm, prema-

ture as it proved, when General Changarnier mobilized the troops
in Paris—to protect the Assembly in his own version but counseling
a coup d'état. Thiers was opposed to this, as was the president at this
point, who was still feeling his way and in still hesitant fashion going
through his apprenticeship of French political ways.

Already in December the Assembly had voted for itself an ambitious program of constitutional legislation, the enactment of which
would have considerably prolonged its existence. But the republican majority was losing its cohesion; much of it was after all made up
of passive acquiescence, the equivalent of the Plain in the 1793
Convention, apt to rally to any determined leadership. As a consequence, the program of constitutional legislation was abandoned,
the electoral law of 1848 was confirmed, and elections for a new
legislative body set for May 13.

*Italian Complications*

One problem did appear, however, before the disbanding of the
Assembly, that gave rise to meaningful debate, harbinger of the
larger discussion of foreign policy in general. The problem grew out
of Italian developments, the course of which must be briefly
recalled.

Although a Sicilian rising in January 1848 had antedated the Parisian, it was the repercussions of the latter that set in motion a train
of European avents. The first half of the century in the Italian peninsula had witnessed agitation that was at once nationalistic and liberal. In either form that agitation was opposed by the established
order: Austria, the paramount power in the peninsula; the Pope,
endowed with a peculiar, universal mission; and the other ruling
princes. Early in 1848 the whole Italian structure seemed to be
collapsing. The month of March witnessed insurrections in Milan
that expelled the Austrians from that city, the proclamation of a
republic in their Venetian domain, and the granting of a constitution
by the King of Piedmont, who in addition went to war against Austria, a war in which even papal forces initially joined.

Though taken by surprise, the Austrians soon recovered. By July
they had defeated the Piedmontese who accepted an armistice, the
moderate terms of which were in part the result of Anglo-French
mediation.

But this was only the first act. In Rome the Pope yielded to liberal
demands by appointing Count Rossi, a man of the Guizot school, as

prime minister, a far-reaching concession considering the nature of the papal regime. But Rossi was murdered and further radical agitation induced the Pope to take refuge in Gaeta, while in February 1849 a republic was proclaimed in Rome, in the management of which Garibaldi and Mazzini joined hands. The following month the Piedmontese unwisely resumed the war against Austria; the only result was a repetition of the defeat of the preceding year, whereupon the Piedmontese king abdicated in favor of his son.

As always, Italian events were of interest to France, whose nonintervention had allowed them to unfold as indicated, the predominance of the Austrian power reasserting itself. But there was another factor this time. The French president was in general sympathetic to the nationalistic urge, to the Italian aspect of it in particular; his early association with the *carbonari* has been mentioned. For that reason, therefore, as well as for the more permanent one of balance-of-power considerations, Italian affairs were of especial interest to the French at this point.

The result was French action in two quarters, the Roman and the Piedmontese. Nothing had come of the French offer of asylum to the Pope, but the government raised the question of the desirability of occupying some Piedmontese territory as a pledge of resistance to possible Austrian demands. This subject was debated in the Assembly on March 31. Thiers, whose criticism of the withdrawal from Ancona was cited by way of example, intervened in the discussion to argue that a clash with Austria ran the risk of enlargement into a European conflagration, and that the French interest was a matter of influence, something that could be defended without resort to war.

Later we shall observe the manner in which, according to Thiers, the French interest should be defended, in Italy and elsewhere in central Europe, and his view of the precise nature of that interest. For the moment, where France was concerned, the Roman situation resulted in confusion. The credits voted by the Assembly were used to send an expeditionary force to Rome, where its leader, General Oudinot, instead of receiving the expected welcome was met by armed resistance. An agreement negotiated with the Roman Republic having been subsequently disavowed by the French government, Oudinot proceeded to take the city by force; this was in June. In rather unexpected fashion the French interest was balancing the Austrian: the Pope was reestablished in his own domain with the help of French bayonets while the Austrians were forcing the surrender of the Venetian Republic. Louis Napoleon, with an eye on the French domestic situation, was not insensitive to the value of Catholic support, though even this is not complete summation of the complexity of his ways.

# CHAPTER 10

# The End of the Republic

I N any case, by the time these events took place, which amounted to the defeat of the revolution in Italy, the French Assembly had dissolved itself and elections had been held for its successor in May. For electoral purposes the forces of order joined hands, with the consequence that they won the consultation, although the forces of the Left retained substantial backing. But an attempted rising in Paris in June, engineered by Ledru-Rollin, was harshly put down by General Changarnier.

The ministry continued to be led by Odilon Barrot, with de Tocqueville at the foreign office. Thiers was not part of it, as he continued not to be for the rest of the life of the Second Republic, but he did not renounce political activity, the record of which will now be briefly outlined.

## I  Thiers Condones Repression

The domestic political course of the Second Republic from this time until its effective demise in 1851 may be summed up as that of a steady and continuing trend in the direction of personal power. Louis Napoleon was a complex man, not the ineffectually innocuous innocent that his early participation in the proceedings of the Assembly had caused many to believe he was. He maneuvered with skill within the new constitutional structure.

The institution of universal suffrage had done little to shift the location of real controls. The more radical tendency, those for whom the Republic meant a new order of things, constituted a real force, though they remained a minority in the country as a whole. Those in charge of affairs, the government and private business, continued to be the same group that had supported the July Monarchy but had in the end brought about its overthrow. Thiers belonged in this group,

103

little concerned with formal nomenclature, therefore willing to accept the Republic.

The consequence of the distribution of forces was thus a clash between the legislative body and the president. The newly elected Assembly first met on May 28. Within two weeks, the clumsy Roman imbroglio caused Ledru-Rollin to introduce a motion that was tantamount to an accusation of the president and his ministers. In the debate on June 12 Thiers defended the government, arguing that the use of force in Rome had been justified since it was a case of the defense of order against the anarchic demagoguery of the Roman Republic.

And he adhered to the same position in October when the government's request of additional credits was under debate.[1] He went as far as justifying the Pope's *motu proprio,* a curious inversion of positions between himself and the president, for the latter was pursuing an ambivalent policy where the Pope was concerned: while desirous of reaping the benefits that his role in having restored the Pope would bring among French Catholic opinion, he also considered that the Pope should introduce real reforms in his domain. Louis Napoleon's policy of seeking moderate change, for which a case of reasonableness could be made, was open to the charge of duplicity.

In any case, especially after the suppression of the above-mentioned abortive demonstration of June 13, the continuing institution of repressive measures characterizes the policy of Louis Napoleon. Let us examine some of the aspects of the operation and Thiers' reaction to it.

## The Press and Education

The position and role of the press had always been subjects close to the heart of journalist Thiers. His intervention in the debate on July 24 on proposed legislation in regard to freedom of the press is revealing of his position at the time and of the degree of his evolution. He sought to define in his speech the proper limits of freedom, which, according to him, should not extend to the advocacy of the destruction of the regime or the incitement to revolt. Not insensitive to the desirability of change, he felt nevertheless that the degree of it that had taken place was excessive.

The field of education has been a battleground on which the

opposite tendencies of the forces of movement and those of conservation, the contending liberal and conservative orientations, have often met in France since the Great Revolution. The central issue has been that of the role of the Church, of private versus public education. It is but one aspect of the more ancient quarrel between the state and the Church, which in France means the Roman. The first Napoleon in his Concordat had gone so far as to acknowledge the undeniable fact that Catholicism was the religion of the majority of the French people, but, feeling, like the Church, that the school is a powerful tool for the molding of minds, he had instituted a system of state control of education. However, owing in part at least to the problems of physical facilities and personnel, Catholic schools after the Restoration continued to play a large part in the training of French youth, training imparted by a variety of congregations, among whom the Jesuits were the most conspicuous.

The issues growing out of the 1848 revolution were essentially two: the organization and the control of education at the primary and at the secondary levels. The conservative elements, the party of order, wished to leave primary education under ecclesiastical control, meaning that the *instituteurs* would not be subject to prefectorial (state) supervision. The entrance of the conservative Falloux in the ministry, in charge of educational affairs, was a point won by the Catholics.

As a member of the commission charged with the preparation of a bill, Thiers opposed free (non paying) elementary education, which he acknowledged was desirable but not *owed* by society to its members, arguing in addition the cost of such an undertaking. His general approach was indicated when he spoke on the subject in the Assembly on January 18, 1850:

After all that we have seen in the last two years, I do not hesitate to confess that I have changed my position. Yes, in the face of the immense dangers that have threatened and continue to threaten society, I may indeed have intended to unite its various defenders, to put an end to the quarrels between the partisans of the state and the partisans of the Church, because both of them, if they understand their interest and their duty, must today be the defenders of society (approving signs from the Right). That has been my intention; but you are going to see how, in order to fulfill it, I have taken the hand of M. de Montalembert[2] in mine without his beliefs or mine having had to suffer from this.

and, again on the same occasion, to emphasize the shift in his position, "it is true that today I do not feel toward the clergy the
jealousies, the fears that I entertained two years ago." This shift he
justified by claiming that "the partisans of the Church, the partisans
of the State . . . are the defenders of society, of society that I believe imperiled, and I have held out my hand to them."[3]

Determined opponent of the Jesuits though he had been, Thiers
had come to see merits in them as defenders of order against the
threats of anarchists and libertarians in general; for that reason he was
led to join hands with Montalembert and Monsignor Dupanloup.[4]
In the discussion the following month of the organization of de-
partmental commissions with supervisory powers over the *instituteurs*, Thiers spoke strongly in favor of an amendment intended
to give the bishops a place on the commissions.[5]

Yet it was not so much that Thiers had changed his fundamental
position as that the new forces that were asserting themselves constituted in his eyes a threat to his unchanging view of the proper
ordering of society, the location of the centers of power in it; put in
different language, Thiers displayed inability to keep up with the
times.

But it is also interesting to note the limitations he would put on
the control of education. This appeared a few days later in a further
discussion of the content of the curriculum of secondary education.
When an amendment was proposed that would have had the effect
of eliminating philosophy from the subjects of instruction, he vigorously opposed that change. As he put it, with perhaps unintended
humor:

> We respect the freedom of the human spirit. . . . Spinoza was assuredly a
> powerful and deplorable genius. If he were living today, we should not
> wish, out of respect for the freedom of the human spirit, to deprive him of
> the right of writing a book; but we should not make him a professor, and we
> should approve the minister who had removed him.[6]

The mass should be properly indoctrinated—and what better than a
religious education could do that?—but their rulers should be free
to exercise their critical minds. In such an approach one may easily
read inconsistency; Thiers would have called it simple reasonableness. Voltaire would have agreed.

The outcome of these debates at the beginning of January 1850
was the enactment of the Falloux law regarded as a great success for

the Catholic position and in that sense another feather in the cap of reaction. While this interpretation is warranted, the effect of the law was not what had been either hoped or feared. In the long run, neither freedom of instruction nor control of education by the Church came to prevail. The real effect was to make French education at once so rigid and so free, and at the elementary level to promote the long war between the curé and the *instituteur*, so characteristic of the French scene. The issue, incidentally, though in updated garb, is still being fought out in France.

### The Social Question. *"La vile multitude"*

Another aspect of the problem of the proper ordering of society is that of the responsibility of the state for social services, in other words what should that rubric cover? Something has been said of the institution of the National Workshops in 1848 and of the failure of that mishandled experiment. But the issue recurred. The Assembly had appointed a committee to look into all aspects of the problem of what now would be called social security and welfare. As rapporteur of the committee Thiers expounded at great length at the end of January 1850 on the results of the committee's deliberations. "The fundamental principle of any society," asserted Thiers, "is that each man is responsible for himself, providing for his needs and those of his family through the resources acquired by or transferred to him."[7] Having posited this basic principle, he went on to examine in detail the three stages of human existence, youth, maturity, and old age.

On the score of responsibility for the care of childhood, for children born out of wedlock in particular, he had some very modern-sounding things to say, though drawing a rather unduly rosy picture of the extent to which society had in the past discharged that responsibility. But where it came to middle age, the active, productive period of life, while agreeing that public works could be of use in offering temporary assistance, he adhered to his denial of the responsibility of the state in realizing such an utopia as the right to work for all. Interestingly, he was in favor of colonization, both at home, in the form of developing backward sections of the country, and abroad, though not too far away from home. The conception of a French empire, an extension of France across the Mediterranean to mid Africa, rather than scattered worldwide like the British, may already be perceived in Thiers' view.

For old age, providence and self-reliance were the best protection, and again the role of the state should remain the minimal one of supervisory regulation; no subsidies to homes for the aged for instance. The whole report is of interest as indicative of the stage of development of social thinking at the time. The emphasis remained on the merits of individual self-reliance; in France as elsewhere this was the heyday of free enterprise.

But in one particular domain, that of protective tariffs, free enterprise did not yet carry the day against protection, although there were those in France who advocated the merits of the English approach. A debate took place on the subject in June 1851, and the long speeches that Thiers delivered on that occasion were gathered together to form, together with an introductory preface, a little volume in which his economic thought was expanded. Thiers was not ignorant of economics, but his outlook was typical of what came to be the cautiously conservative one of French capital in contrast with the more adventurous British. One can already see in his case the makings of the economic thinking that came to be characteristic of France as the century passed, an attitude that put greater emphasis on safety than on the greater returns that may go with greater risk. If there are merits in this cautious tendency, it is also responsible for the relative decline of France, in the economic as in other domains, from second place among the important nations of the world to a lower position. It was consistent on Thiers' part to have favored a cautious policy of railway building and to have been critical of the speculation that was rife in connection with that activity, as he was also critical of the too loose control of state finance.

The spring of 1850 registered a further success of the forces of reaction. As a result of the rising of the preceding June, a number of deputies, thirty-one, had been tried, found guilty, and deprived of their seats. In the by-elections for their replacement, although only twenty-one members of the Left were returned, the result had the effect of alarming the conservative elements to the extent of inducing a fall in the quotation of state funds and a somewhat panicky withdrawal of savings.

The answer of these perhaps unduly alarmed conservative elements was an attempt to modify the franchise, restricting universal suffrage, a dangerous innovation in the eyes of many representatives. A frontal attack on the new dispensation would have been difficult, but a tangential one was contained in a piece of legislation that introduced residential requirements. The debate of the proposal, in May 1850, was heated. While Victor Hugo and Lamartine attacked the proposed restriction, that, interestingly, the president also opposed, Thiers spoke vigorously in its favor, resorting to a somewhat sophistical distinction between the people and the multitude, the mob. This was the occasion on which, in the heat of debate, on May 24, he allowed his temper to get the better of his judgment, referring to "the multitude, the vile multitude." Though he meant this, the phrase was politically incautious; he sought to give a softening explanation, but it would subsequently return to plague him.[8] The project was adopted, with the consequence of reducing the electorate by about one third. Some six million voters were a good many more than the 200,000 of the preceding regime, but one had to be content with small blessing.

## II   *The Coup d'État*

The conservative majority of the Assembly and the president were not too far apart, certainly where it came to muzzling and suppressing what they both saw as the threatening excesses of radical republicanism. But the majority was divided, the Royalist factions in it, Legitimists and Orleanists, unable to agree, despite some efforts in which Thiers himself was involved, to bridge the gap between them. Dislike and suspicion of the president were widespread in the Assembly, a sentiment that he reciprocated. And there were those who, again like Thiers, still thought best the arrangements of the preceding regime, a middle course between rule by "the vile multitude" and the abuses of personal power.

In the conflict that was developing, Louis Napoleon maneuvered with skill, making use of methods that have a very modern touch though they have been much perfected since; Louis Napoleon understood the possibilities of publicity and public relations. His travels through the country, his ambiguous declarations, were designed to make himself known while appealing to all shades of opinion. The cry of *Vive Napoléon! Vive l'Empereur!* began to be heard on occasion, though there were also countercries, especially in the urban centers. The raising of this cry at the military review at Satory in October created a sensation and alarm in the Assembly. The ostensibly correct behavior of the commander of the Paris garrison, General Changarnier, irritated the president, who entertained the possibility of his dismissal while he effected changes in the ministry.

The locus of the ultimate control of the military—not a new issue—reappeared as the subject of an intense debate when the Assembly met again in January, in connection with a resolution critical of the ministry, hence at one remove of the president. Thiers intervened in a long speech[9] in which, after examining the British and the American constitutional arrangements, he advocated, as on many other occasions, the former as the more suitable model for France. Going on to explain the reasons for his support of the July Monarchy, he acknowledged a possible misjudgment on his part, justifying his role in having brought about its downfall, and professed loyalty to the Republic. Summing up the issue of the moment, he ended with a since-famous peroration:

> . . . there are today only two powers in the state, the executive power and the legislative power.
> If the Assembly yields today only one is left. And when there will be only one the form of the government will be changed; the name, the title will come . . . when they will come, that matters little; but that which you say today you do not want, if the Assembly yields, you will have this very day; I repeat, there is only one power left, the word will come when it will be wanted . . . the Empire is made.

The censure motion was carried by a vote of 415 to 286.

Thiers' warning was fully warranted, and from that point, although it took the rest of the year to effect the fundamental change, the drift of things was clear and in one direction only.

Leaving aside various minor issues that arose, parliamentary and ministerial maneuvers in which Thiers played some part, there was one that proved to be the final turning point. In the spring an agitation began for a revision of the constitution, the question being that of making possible the reelection of the president, who meantime was actively pursuing his campaign of publicity, increasingly casting himself in the role of defender of the people, even against their representatives. Had they not after all disenfranchised one third of the electorate?

But revision of the constitution was difficult, having purposely been made so through the requirement of a three quarters majority, while the supporters of revision when it came to a vote in the Assembly could muster no more than a simple majority. That vote, which closed the door to the establishment of personal power through legal devices, was what decided Louis Napoleon in favor of the resort to force, a coup d'état. Talk of that possibility was rife as certain military preparations and administrative reshufflings were increasingly pointing to its likelihood. There is neither space nor need to dwell on these preparations, on the whole well coordinated, and on certain delays which resulted in finally setting the date as December 2, the anniversary of Austerlitz.

The management of the new 18th of Brumaire bears some resemblance to that of the earlier performance, on the whole an easily successful operation in which legal parliamentary opposition caused no more than momentary hesitation and delay. A last-minute debate in the Assembly in November, in which Thiers intervened again, over the perennial question of to whom the armed forces owed allegiance, did little more than emphasize the divisions and the ineffectualness of that body. Quite logically, the leaders of what might be expected to be continued opposition were secured. Being one of them, Thiers was arrested early on the morning of December 2 and seemed to have felt some concern for his safety. But Louis Napoleon was not an especially cruel man and Thiers was after all a well-entrenched member of the Establishment, the very antithesis of a doctrinaire radical, hardly one to resort to an appeal to the vile multitude, an endeavor in which Louis Napoleon himself could perform with greater congeniality and skill.

There was, in Paris and elsewhere in the country, opposition to the coup. Insofar as that opposition took popular form it was thoroughly put down, to the accompaniment of numerous arrests, followed by trials, prison, and deportation sentences. But overall, and allowing for the full use of official pressure in the subsequent voting on the consitutional issue, Louis Napoleon's request that he be confirmed in his position as president and entrusted with the task of drafting a new constitution was overwhelmingly endorsed by the French people.

Thiers need not have feared for his personal safety. He was released after four days, but simultaneously banished from the country. He arrived in Brussels on December 12, beginning a period of extensive travel. His career in French politics was momentarily ended, and though he kept abreast of their unfolding he did not again take an active part in French affairs for a full decade. Leaving the course of French politics aside, save as it may have to be referred to an occasion, we shall follow Thiers through his decade of political retirement.

CHAPTER 11

# The Second French Empire

## I  *Exile and Return*

THIERS' dramatic warning in his speech in the Assembly on January 17, 1851 was only a little premature, for it took another whole year before the name of the regime was formally changed, although the coup d'état marked the real turning point in constitutional arrangements.

Meanwhile, he was himself driven into exile, which he put to good purpose, spending some months in extensive travel. His well-established reputation, his former place in French affairs, insured him easy entrée in society and to those who held positions of power, the Establishment of the day, wherever his peregrinations took him. He did not tarry long in Brussels, where his recent role in his country's politics caused him to adopt an attitude of reserved discretion; Thiers was never a popular agitator of the Mazzini stamp. For that reason he did not meet King Leopold, who felt, on his side, that he must adopt a cautious position vis-à-vis his powerful French neighbor; but that shrewd and intelligent monarch expressed his regret at the missed opportunity to discuss the situation with Thiers.

From Brussels Thiers went in January to London where he was well received, in fact lionized, in English social circles and, as was ever his wont, put his time to good use in familiarizing himself with things English in general, institutions, and monuments. He was very impressed by the ceremony of the opening of Parliament, and what he had an opportunity to observe confirmed his high regard for the ways of British politics. He compared notes with many prominent figures, and this stay was the occasion for his acquaintance with Nassau Senior, whose later reports of their frank discussions over a number of years constitute a highly informative source[1] on Thiers' views of current events as well as on his share in earlier ones.

112

While he found exile burdensome, return to France was still barred. He left England in April, passing through Belgium again, then up the Rhine, through Switzerland, into Italy where he proceeded as far as Naples, new territory for him, always visiting places of interest, museums, and antiquities, on which he made careful notes. Then he went north again to Switzerland, where his family rejoined him in June. His exile was not to last much longer. Louis Napoleon was not a cruel or vindictive man, and for that matter might not Thiers be brought around to accepting the new regime? Dedicated to liberty as he was, his dislike of revolution gave law and order a high priority in his scheme of values. In any case a decree of August 7 put an end to his banishment, as well as to that of some others, and he shortly returned to his Parisian home to become once more a familiar figure in the salons of the capital where the leading political, literary, and social figures of the day were wont to congregate. He himself, endowed by now with substantial property—he achieved, among other things, the directorship of the Anzin coal mines, an enterprise in which he had profitably invested—could reciprocate entertainment in the upper bourgeois surroundings of his own *hôtel* on the Place St. Georges.

## II   *Advent and Nature of the Imperial Regime*

The coup d'état, followed within three weeks by a plebiscite, had the effect of placing the president in a position of totally unchecked power. Arbitrary and absolute as the regime may have been, it yet must be given some framework of legality, which was the meaning of the grant of the power of constitution drafting. That task was done with expedition, not to say haste, and by mid January France was endowed with a new constitution, in considerable measure a replica of that of the Year VIII, the instrument that had paved the way for the dictatorial position of the first Napoleon. Like the earlier document, the constitution of 1852 was characterized by the fragmentation of power among the legislative bodies, meaning that the real seat of power would reside in the executive.

In February elections took place for the *Corps Législatif*, a consultation that may be put down as a mere formality or a farce; out of 261 members 256 were supporters of the government. Louis Napoleon was a very modern man, fully aware of the possibilities of state control by means of a variety of devices and pressures, an early practicer of the wiles of demagoguery, a usage that our own time has since so much perfected. The press was severely restricted, not so much by outright censorship as through its liability to penalties that might follow a warning; the possibilities of "voluntary censorship" have also been perfected.

The contrived official pressures, the influence of the *préfets* being put to good use, were the prelude to the realization of Thiers' prediction. Louis Napoleon travelled extensively about the country, both to make himself better known and to test the temper of the people. Increasingly the cry *Vive L'Empereur!* was heard, though often a command performance. Contrived as it all may have been, there is also no denying that the Napoleonic name carried considerable appeal among large numbers for whom the passage of forty years had effected the selective process that frequently enhances the memory of the past. The speech delivered on October 9 in Bordeaux, where Haussmann was *préfet* and had organized an enthusiastic reception, was the harbinger of impending change, after which Louis Napoleon returned to Paris, where a triumphal reception greeted him.

The next month a *senatus consultum* proposed the formal reestablishment of the empire, that another plebiscite endorsed by an overwhelming vote of nearly eight million against a mere quarter of a million; official pressure alone could hardly have procured such a result. By a decree of December 2 France once more became an empire, Louis Napoleon assuming the name of Napoleon III.

There was significance in the numeral, for it implied continuity with the earlier Napoleonic regime and endorsement of what it had stood for. And certainly one thing that the rule of the first Napoleon had meant had been war. French events were of prime interest to all Europe which had been watching them with concern. That is the reason why, fully aware of the question that the restoration of the empire in France raised for all Europe, Louis Napoleon had declared in the Bordeaux speech that "some people think: the Empire means war; but I say: the Empire means peace. It means peace because France wishes it, and when France is satisfied the world is tranquil." Reassuring words to the outside, but, especially in the light of the recent course of events, how dependable? Deeds speak louder than words.

Actually, the reassurance was honestly meant and Napoleon III entertained, initially at least, no aggressive designs. Nonetheless, Thiers, who was in England again in November, declared to Senior that he expected war in the near future.[2] Though Thiers himself was also in favor of peace, he was not averse to extensive European rearrangements. He thought that, in connection with the 1848 disturbances, France could have acquired Mainz and Savoy, promoted an Italian federation, while Austria could have been compensated in the Balkans, a move that would have the additional merit of enlisting her in the containment of Russian expansion. There will be occasion to return to these schemes. For the rest, Thiers held a very dim view of the new French emperor's abilities, and he had unhesitatingly turned down the attempts that Louis Napoleon had made, while still president, to have him join the government.

### III  *Thiers and the Authoritarian Empire*

The period until 1860 is usually labelled that of the authoritarian empire, a description justified by the repressive nature of the regime, of which the status of the press is an accurate measure, as well as the government's interference with the electoral process. On these two issues Thiers had consistently held views sufficiently strong to account for his refusal to participate in the politics of the day, let alone lend the government the support that his participation in it would have meant.

This did not mean a lack of interest in the course of events, an interest that his acquaintance with many in the ruling group made it easy for him to sustain. Nor were his relations with the political establishment characterized by doctrinaire inflexibility and unfriendliness, even with the emperor himself; Napoleon III took note of an accident that befell Thiers—a broken arm—in 1855 and conveyed his sympathy on that occasion. Critical of certain aspects of the regime though he might be, Thiers could not after all overlook the important accomplishment that was the maintenance of social order. The emperor also took note of the *History of the Consulate and the Empire*, not a surprising thing considering the authorship and the subject. But Thiers resisted all blandishments to rally the regime, even when the suggestion that he do so came from other than French quarters, Lady Holland, for example, and even Bismarck on one occasion.[3]

Apparently he did not feel, at least not yet, that even in opposition he would exert a significant influence. So, apart from an active social life and further travel—he was in Belgium, Germany, and England again in 1856—he pursued with assiduity his historical

work. Yet he found political retirement burdensome, for politics had
been the very stuff of his activity. As he put it to Senior, when the
latter was sojourning in Paris:

At my age, and with my health, I am now in my very greatest vigor, and
my career is suddenly cut short. In a country in which, if he had not robbed
it of its liberty, I ought to be foremost, I am nothing.[4]

And upon Senior pointing out his political record so far and his
current literary accomplishments, he went on:

Writing is a poor thing after action. I would give ten successful histories
for one successful session or for one successful campaign. The loss of power,
I mean not of place, for that is nothing, but of influence, the loss of the
means of directing the destinies of one's country—is bitter at all times; but
it is doubly bitter now, when France is engaged in a struggle, and is supported by an alliance which has been the dream of all my life. . . . To have
concurred with Lord Clarendon in directing the united policy of France and
England would have been the glorious reward of a life of toil.[5]

There is no reason to doubt the authenticity of these feelings.

### Two Contrasting Appraisals: the Crimea and Italy

Senior had come to Paris with the intention of proceeding to
Algeria, but the interest of the local scene caused him to remain in
the French capital. For France and England were at war jointly
against Russia. Thiers' forecast of war shortly after the advent of the
Second Empire was thus proved right, though war had come about
in a manner and over an issue other than he had expected.

This is not the place to give a detailed account of the origins and
course of the Crimean War. Broadly speaking, it grew out of the
constant Russian drive toward the Straits, a drive in resisting which
England and France could agree, though in this particular respect
the English interest had primacy over the French. More immediately, the war grew out of the relatively insignificant "quarrel
of the monks," the rivalry between French and Russian interests in
the respective protection of Catholic and Greek Orthodox
coreligionaries in the Ottoman Empire, more specifically in
Jerusalem, where a highly complex set of arrangements prevailed.

It was a very small issue, but Tsar Nicholas had snubbed the
upstart French emperor and prestige was involved so that the situa-

tion was allowed to escalate into unnecessary conflict. Napoleon III did not want war, but a diplomatic success seemed desirable, especially in the defense of Catholic rights. Neither did the Tsar want war, but in contrast with 1840 his attempt to effect an arrangement with England failed, and in addition Stratford de Redcliffe, the British representative in Constantinople, took a strong anti-Russian stance and some initiatives of his own.[6] To make a long story short, after a series of moves and countermoves by the various participants, and some futile negotiations in Vienna, Turkey declared war on Russia in October 1853. It took almost another five months before Britain and France joined in the war.

The Crimean War was a rather wretched performance, from the standpoint at least of the quality of managment of the participants, for all that it produced heroics—the charge of the Light Brigade and MacMahon on the Malakoff tower—as well as Florence Nightingale. But, in the reckoning, the Russians were defeated on their home ground, a fact that the convenient demise of the Tsar made it easier for them to accept.

The bungled episode was settled at the Congress of Paris in March 1856. The congress was a brilliant occasion, replete with festivities in which the Russians were included, further enhanced where Napoleon III was concerned by the foresight of Empress Eugénie in choosing that particular moment to present him with an heir, a cause for universal congratulations while the congress took a recess. More seriously, the episode—the war and the congress—undoubtedly redounded to the prestige of the French imperial regime.[7] But it is Thiers' reaction to these events that is our primary interest.

That reaction was one of unqualified enthusiasm, for what had happened fitted to perfection two positions that he held very strongly: the importance of keeping Russia out of the Mediterranean, in which respect he was more English than French, and even more the achievement of a joint Anglo-French policy. On many subsequent occasions, when speaking in the *Corps Législatif* on foreign policy matters after he had become a member of that body, he returned to the theme of his approval of the Crimean War.

But he also used those occasions to point to a contrast, for he thoroughly disapproved of the war against Austria at the end of the decade. Mention has been made of his sympathy for the Italian struggle for liberty and of the manner in which he would have dealt with the Italian situation.[8] In that case and from his standpoint things had gone altogether wrong.

The Italian case was a typical instance of nineteenth-century nationalism. Leaving aside the complexities and the historical background of the fragments that made up the Italian peninsula, especially after the Napoleonic wars the feeling grew that looked to the making of a united Italy. The agitation for it was the *Risorgimento*. On how to accomplish this end and the form it should take there were different views that it would take too long to retail.[9] But with the advent of Count Cavour, a typical nineteenth-century liberal not very different from Thiers, to the Prime Ministership of Piedmont following the 1848 disturbances the Piedmontese leadership asserted itself.[10]

Cavour, though himself a member of the nobility, rather fitted the characterization of bourgeois. A modern man, aware of the forces that were molding the world of his time, industry and commerce, he chose England and its rising business class, as well as English institutions, as his preferred models. But England was far away, and though there the Italian cause was popular, little more than sympathy was forthcoming. Bayonets were needed to undo the Austrian dominance, and those that Italy herself could furnish were insufficient for the task, as 1848 and 1849 had conclusively shown. Who else but France could furnish them?

The problem was how to enlist the French. In the effort to do this Cavour was assisted by the French emperor's general sympathy for the nationalistic urge, the Italian in particular. The outcome of these circumstances was the plan, or plot, that the two men elaborated in their meeting at Plombières in July 1858. Cavour would see to it that Austria put herself in the position of aggressor, thus enabling France to come to the assistance of Piedmont, as provided in the defensive alliance. The formation of a Kingdom of Northern Italy, adding the Austrian possessions, Lombardy and Venetia, to the Savoyard kingdom, would be Piedmont's reward, while France would gain Savoy and Nice, ostensibly a further application of the principle of ethnic nationality, and would be rewarded by the replacement of Austrian influence with her own in the peninsula.

Initially all went according to plan. The war that broke out in the spring of 1859 was a success for the Franco-Sardinian combination. But second thoughts, and a Prussian mobilization, induced Napoleon III to meet his Austrian counterpart, Francis Joseph, and put an end to the conflict with the armistice the two signed at Villafranca on July 11. Austria would cede Lombardy—to France, which would turn it over to Piedmont—but retain Venetia; Cavour was not even consulted. But other Italian developments occurred that could not be arrested. The whole political structure of the peninsula collapsed, and before 1860 was out, its entirety, save for a small territory around Rome, was joined into one, the Kingdom of Italy being proclaimed in May 1861.

There is no question that, by going to war against Austria and defeating her, France had made all this possible. She can therefore be said to have made Italy. But what had she done for herself in the process? She had at one point abandoned her ally and in the final outcome was responsible for preventing the total completion of Italian unity, through her insistence on the independence of the Pope in Rome, and through allowing the Austrians to remain in Venice. She had also made possible the rise of a substantial new state on her border. This outcome, to be sure, may be taken as confirming Bismarck's judgment that the French emperor's heart was better than his head, but as head of the French state his first care should have been the protection of the French interest. The acquisition of Nice and Savoy seemed dubious compensation.

Thiers saw more clearly than Napoleon III where the French interest lay; just as he had been enthusiatically in favor of the war against Russia, he thought the one against Austria a mistake. Nationalist as he may have been in his own country, and fully capable of understanding and even sympathizing with the desire of other nations for greatness, he also thought that the current tendency, its Mazzinian form in particular, to base nationality on linguistic affinity was absurd. There were French-speaking people outside of France, in Belgium and Switzerland for example, but that would hardly justify French annexationist claims in those countries. The tradition of diversity in the Italian case justified the persistence in separateness of the distinct Italian states, a consideration equally valid in the Germanic world. The Austrian state was multinational, but this was not an argument for its destruction, for Austria was an essential component of the European equilibrium, for the preservation of which the existence of small states was indispensable.

The making of a united Italy was a disturbance of that equilibrium, one particularly inimical to the French interest, which had traditionally sought to maintain the fragmentation of mid Europe.

Thiers would express these same views with even greater forceful-
ness in the second half of the 1860s, after he had resumed an active
role in politics and when his dire forecasts were about to be realized.

Yet there was a fundamental flaw in his whole position, for the
nationalistic force, especially in mid Europe, confronted France
with a dilemma for which neither Thiers nor anyone else in France
could supply an adequate answer. Merely to oppose the force was
tantamount to taking a position against the trend of historic development, a trend that there might be good reason to bemoan but
that could hardly be resisted, and certainly not denied, as events
have conclusively shown. Napoleon III's general sympathy for
nationalism was in some ways a more far-seeing approach, though
he bungled his relations with it. The problem went far deeper, for it
was that of how French power could accommodate itself to the rise
of other powers, a condition that simply could not be reconciled
with the continuance of France's primacy on the continent.

The fact remains that France did not have to make Italy at this
particular point, that some aspects of her policy are aptly characterized by the French phrase, *travailler pour le roi de Prusse*, and
that if Thiers had no ultimate answer he was far-sighted and his
criticisms were well founded.

## IV  *How History Should be Written*

Here we must pause to consider the work and place of Thiers as
an historian. The success and influence of his *History of the French
Revolution* have been indicated. Having completed it, Thiers went
on to deal with its sequel, the Napoleonic episode. The result was
the twenty-volume *History of the Consulate and the Empire*.

The writing of this major undertaking filled two decades. Thiers
began to prepare for it in 1841, after his fall from office, collecting
documentary material, and, as was his wont, acquainting himself on
the spot with many of the scenes of action throughout mid Europe
and in Spain. Though many of the archival sources, German and
English in particular, were not available to him, he had access to a
great deal that he industriously sifted.

The first two volumes appeared in 1845, followed by a steady
stream thereafter, until the work was completed in 1862. Like its
predecessor it proved an enormous success that brought handsome
financial rewards, and the critical reception was also generally favorable, though there were those, Taine and Tocqueville among them,

who expressed marked reservations.[11] The work certainly contributed to establish an image of Napoleon in France, but to credit it with the creation of the Napoleonic legend would be an exaggeration; that legend was already prosperous in 1840.

The twelfth volume, which appeared in 1855, was introduced by a lengthy preface, "Considerations on History in General and on the Manner of Writing it," in which Thiers expounded his views on the craft; it is a highly interesting and very relevant disquisition. By present-day standards Thiers' views would undoubtedly be called by some old fashioned; cliometrics and psychohistory had not entered the practice and the vocabulary of the day, but that is hardly a serious limitation, for the value is open to question of the contribution made by the attempt to use pseudoscientific categories and jargon in a discipline that remains in large part literary art.

But if the novel may sometimes convey an equally good, or even better, understanding of a personality or of the essential spirit of a time than formal historical writing, history as understood by Thiers must remain strictly bound to fact, "scientific" to that extent—the impact of the exact sciences, the worship of fact, was profound on the age. This is not, however, Marxist objectivity, no less naive than the belief in the possibility of exact scientific procedure in the social domain. But Thiers would have had no quarrel with Leopold von Ranke's *wie-es-eigentlich-gewesen* ideal. Ranke, incidentally, had esteem for Thiers and his work.

There are, according to Thiers, many ways of writing history, but "the essential quality, preferable to all others, that must distinguish the historian, . . . is intelligence."[12] This requirement he could not overstress, though it should also be pointed out that the word carries in the French language somewhat different overtones from those in the English; the more restricted French meaning puts the emphasis on *intellectual* understanding, leaving less room for adaptability to circumstances, in which fact one may see the merits and the limitations of a characteristically French approach.

The historian must divest himself of passion, something to which "the profound knowledge of men" can contribute. Guicciardini and Frederick the Great are cited as examples of writers who successfully overcame the influence of highly different temperaments.

If by disposition [wrote Thiers] you are indulgent or severe, something of that characteristic will appear, not in the fundamentals, but in the form, of your judgments. You may be sad, like Guicciardini or Tacitus, but like them you will display the justice that derives from the height of rationality. I thus come back to my original assertion: if you have an understanding of human affairs, you will have the requisite quality to expound them with clarity, diversity, depth, order and justice.

But, again, the absence of passion must not mean the elimination of feeling. For history is also art, and Thiers draws parallels from painting, Raphael's for example, which could depict idealized madonnas as well as Popes with warts and all. "History is the portrait, as the madonnas of Raphael are the poetry." Hence also the importance of style, which must be suited to the subject, but play the role of the perfect mirror, of the existence of which the looker remains unaware.

These are no doubt ideal requirements, and it is interesting to observe how they are implemented in Thiers' account of the Napoleonic epic. Where style is concerned, the work has passed the test of time. Thiers was much interested in military matters and took great pains to familiarize himself with the locale of engagements. His detailed and lengthy description of battles, Marengo to cite but one example, and his account of the Russian campaign, the retreat from Moscow in particular, still make fascinating reading. But Thiers cast his net wider, paying considerable attention to matters economic and financial, where his own competence was considerable, though paying less attention to institutions.

For all his dispassionateness, Thiers held strong views on certain things, a fact he did not attempt to conceal or deny. "I do not say that one will not find in it [my account] my personal opinions: I should feel very ashamed if one did not, but one will find them in the last volume to be the same as in the first." The claim to consistency may on the whole be granted, even though some influence appears of the periods during which the writing was done: the July Monarchy, his true love though he was in opposition to it in the 1840s, the troubled passage of the Second Republic, the time of the authoritarian empire. Throughout it all, nevertheless, Thiers continued a staunch adherent to the principles of 1789, the regime of bourgeois control, the rule of the qualified and the property holders.

Lacking space for a lengthier discussion of Thiers' historical work, we shall use as summary some further quotations:

Here is an extraordinary young man, who, following ten years of horrible anarchy, appears before his contemporaries covered with glory! Through the operation of the very laws of his country, laws ignored and commanding but scant respect, but laws nevertheless, he rises to supreme power. Through his wisdom, his prudence, his benefactions, his miracles, he becomes the delight of his country and the admiration of the world. But the heady wine of success soon goes to his head; he assails Europe, crushes it, subjects it, oppresses it, driving it to rebellion against him, falling at last amidst incomparable glory into an abyss where he drags France with himself! How judge this prodigious life? Was he right, was he wrong in seizing a sceptre that all invited him to grasp? What man would have resisted such temptation? Does not his fault rather lie in the use he made of supreme authority? But if one exonerates the usurpation of power, criticizing only the use made of it, does not one thereby forget that the violent manner of taking it contained the seed of its violent use?

Thiers could not resist the feeling of national pride. Yet he could also judge with severity the mistakes of inordinate pride, as well as recognize the validity of the claims of some at least of Napoleon's opponents—Metternich whom he admired, though less so Wellington. And in the last analysis he drew a moral from the tale, one in keeping with his own political predilections:

Here is the result of long reflection: it is to believe that if governments sometimes need prodding, more often they stand in need of being restrained; that if sometimes they lean toward inaction, more often, when it comes to politics or war expenditure, their tendency is to undertake too much and not to be deterred by a little embarrassment. To be sure one may add: but who will check this liberty intended to control the power of a single individual? Without any hesitation I answer: all. I know that a country may sometimes go astray, and I have seen it happen, but it does this less often and less completely than one man alone.

Or again:

Thus in this great life [Napoleon's] from which soldiers, administrators, politicians can learn so much, let citizens in turn learn this: the country must never be surrendered to one man, whatever the man, whatever the circumstances.

Coming to the end of this long tale of our triumphs and reverses, that is the last cry that rises from my heart, a sincere cry that I should like to reach the hearts of all Frenchmen, in order to convince them all that liberty must never be yielded, and that in order not to yield it, it must never be abused.

Thiers was an undeviating believer in the fundamentals of the democratic practice, at least in the initial French revolutionary version of it. We shall soon have occasion to see him implementing his convictions. In 1862 his history was done and he was about to reenter his even more beloved field of active politics, in opposition again, reinterating Cassandra-like warnings of impending disaster that were to prove only too accurate. We shall now follow him through the events that provided a suitable climax to a very full career.

### CHAPTER 12

# The Return to Politics

## I   The Meaning of Liberty

*The Liberal Empire*
    The decade of the 1860s is usually characterized as that of
the liberal empire, meaning a changing orientation of the regime
away from dictatorial practice. Napoleon III, still today a controversial personality, was neither an evil nor a stupid man. But he lacked
the quality of decisiveness, with the consequence that he contrived
to achieve the opposite results of those intended. His sympathy for
nationalism in general may well be regarded as forward looking; it
represented at least recognition and acceptance of one of the main
trends of his time. But his management of the Italian situation
earned him little thanks from that quarter, while it aroused the
enmity of French Catholics who felt, quite rightly, that he was
largely responsible for the Pope's plight. It was an odd state of affairs
when the conservative forces were becoming dissatisfied with the
regime for its pursuit of politics of which the liberal opposition
tended to approve. The same applied to the Cobden treaty with
England.[1]
    The outcome of this situation was a relaxation of controls. In
November 1860 the representative bodies regained the right to vote
an address in reply to the speech from the throne, and the full
publicity of their proceedings was also restored; a year later a fuller
discussion of governmental finances was likewise granted. It all
amounted to a revival of political activity, heretofore almost completely stifled.
    The elections of May 1863 were a turning point, when despite the
unusual pressure for the return of official candidates the opposition
managed to receive two million votes out of some 7,500,000. In the
department of the Seine eight Republicans were elected, the re-

125

maining seat going to Thiers, for whom this marked the reentry into
a familiar and beloved field of action. He lost no time in asserting
the position of leadership in the opposition to which his past record
entitled him.

The opening speech from the throne in November 1863 was
answered with a proposed address of complete approval, drafted by
Morny,[2] the discussion of which began with the opening of the new
year. On January 11 Thiers delivered a long, eloquent, and significant speech that amounted to a renewed profession of faith. He
was not totally opposed to the regime, but considered that certain
modifications of it could be effected that would make it one of true
liberty in accordance with his own understanding of the term. These
reforms should meet five requirements: freedom of the individual—the elimination of arbitrary proceedings; freedom of the
press; freedom of the electoral process—no official candidates; parliamentary freedom—unfettered debate; and, finally, ministerial responsibility.

As he put it, "once the legality of the country's government has
been accepted, there are two things one is entitled to ask of it: order
and freedom." Thiers remained consistent in insisting on what he
regarded as fundamentals, to which he attached greater importance
than to outward form; that was why he had been able to accept the
constitutional monarchy (his own preference), the Second Republic,
and now the Empire, which he wanted to see evolve in the direction
of constitutional rule.

He returned to the charge three days later, during the discussion
of an amendment to the address, this time concentrating his attack
on the official candidacies, an abuse of which he gave ample and
telling illustrations. The desirability of centralized government for
France, in contrast with the different condition of Britain, he accepted, but cautioned against the abuse of the facilities that such a
condition put in the hands of the government.

There is no room to examine the various occasions on which
Thiers returned to the same theme, persistence being the only word
that can be used to characterize his behavior. He stated his views
once more a year later, in March 1865,[3] in connection again with the
discussion of the address in reply to the speech from the throne that
opened the session, a speech which to a point attempted to be a
reply to his own of January 1864. He repeated the performance in
February 1866[4] when he used the usual occasion of the discussion of

the address to expatiate on the principles of 1789, which, he insisted, the first article of the constitution of 1852 had confirmed, sovereignty residing in the people; the only problem lay in the deficient application of that principle.

In another connection, of which further mention will have to be made,[5] he attacked "the lack of control over our government," which he attributed to the absence of ministerial responsibility. The gradual liberalization of the regime, the increasing relaxation of official controls, he found insufficient, as when he defended again in January 1868[6] the freedom of the press in another eloquent discourse, insisting that unhampered thought, hence disputation, was the basis of civilization and the very condition of progress.

To the very end, in 1870, Thiers kept insisting, expressing himself very freely in the *Corps Législatif*, where the debate was sometimes not devoid of humor, as when it degenerated into a semantic issue: was Thiers advocating limited change or was he challenging the fundamentals of the constitution? What else was he doing? Yet the trend was unmistakably in the direction he desired. The elections of May 1869 returned a small republican core, and in the face of growing opposition the emperor yielded; the close of the year found Émile Ollivier at the head of the ministry. Might not Thiers' advocacy of gradual evolution have been realized had not foreign complications rendered meaningless that possibility?

Before dealing with the Franco-Prussian War and Thiers' very important role in it and especially in its aftermath, mention must be made of his views and position on two subjects: economic and financial affairs and foreign policy.

## II   *Sound Finance and Free Enterprise*

Good bourgeois that he was, and personally successful in the management of his own fortune, Thiers had a healthy respect for economic and financial soundness. His first intervention in the *Corps Législatif*, after his election to that body in 1863, was in fact on the score of the public debt. On this, as on other occasions,[7] when he spoke on the subject of the state's finances, he consistently took the position, the same as he had taken during the July Monarchy, that the budget was purposely contrived in an endeavor to conceal the true dimensions of expenditures. He had a point, for various disbursements were normally placed under special rubrics, thereby diminishing the ostensible figure of costs. Nevertheless, the amounts involved were not so large as to constitute a threat to the solidity of the country's finances. The period of the Second Empire as a whole was one of economic expansion and the country could without difficulty carry a load of increasing debt, not impairing the soundness of either state finance or the currency. Total expenditure ranged between 1,500,000,000 and 2,500,000,000 francs, amounts that the resources of the country could easily sustain.

At the same time it remains true that economic growth was already showing signs of slackening, in the sense at least that the rate of it was not as high as that of other countries. England, the initial home of industry, still maintained primacy over all by a considerable margin, be it in production or commerce or the availability of capital, but France, which had held second place in the industrial domain, was slipping to a lower position. By the time of the Franco-Prussian War, what was to become Germany was beginning to forge ahead economically, as it was in population, the French approaching a point of virtual stability.

Thiers had studied economics and finance with care, but his outlook may be described as unprogressive. He kept stressing the differences between Britain and France, the manner in which their respective economies had developed, and insisted that the English model was not applicable to his own country. For that reason he never deviated from a strong protectionist position and returned again and again to attacks on the Cobden-Chevalier treaty of 1860, a move in the direction of freer trade. That economic agreement had been Napoleon III's personal accomplishment in the face of opposition of much of the French industrial community.

No doubt France was, and is, unusually self-contained for a country of her dimensions, with a better balanced economy than Britain for example; but to insist on the merits of that situation was tantamount to resisting the economic trend of the modern world and therefore, by implication at least, to accepting a diminishing position. Yet Thiers insisted that France should persist in her role of producer of quality and luxury goods. He was not unaware of certain disadvantages that such a position entailed, the decline of the merchant marine for example, a condition he regretted but which could in his view be remedied by other means. The speeches he delivered in the *Corps Législatif* on matters economic were well informed and closely reasoned, yet on balance, to repeat, represented an unprogressive outlook. In this respect Thiers must be seen as an authentic spokesman of the dominant trend of France's economic practice, one that has only recently been undergoing modernization.

It is characteristic of authoritarian regimes that they indulge in public works on a large scale. The second French empire was no exception to this rule, the outstanding illustration of which is the modern face of Paris, in large measure the work of Baron Haussmann; but on a smaller scale similar changes took place in other French cities as well. Thiers took a considerable interest in this activity, one in which he himself had had a directing hand while holding ministerial office under Louis Philippe. But here again he was critical of the dimensions of the undertaking and of its rising costs, a situation that brings to mind our own current experience of the normally escalating costs of construction projects,[8] not to mention his critical appraisal of certain specific aspects of Haussmann's plan.

### 111 *Foreign Policy: Wherein Lies the French Interest?*

The first Napoleonic performance had given an exaggerated picture of the dimensions and capabilities of French power. Nevertheless, France generally continued to be granted first place among continental powers. In retrospect especially, indications of relative decline, demographic and economic, can be perceived during the first half of the nineteenth century, though to contemporaries they were less obvious. The real central problem of French foreign policy at mid century was that of maintaining position.

Aggressive intent was not the answer, nor was it the policy of the French emperor, but two conditions would combine to bring about his ultimate downfall and with it that of France. Napoleon III was ever alert to possibilities of European rearrangements—a European congress was a pet idea of his that he repeatedly kept advocating out of which some advantage might be gained, though in peaceable fashion; fertile in proposals and schemes, he contrived to create alarm abroad and above all to convey the impression of an intriguing, undependable meddler. The other circumstance was less within his control, arising from developments that had their roots in central European conditions, though he could have had a legitimate say and exercised an influence on the course of their unfolding as well. On the eve of the Austro-Prussian War in 1866, while negotiating an alliance with Italy, Bismarck cautioned the Italian ambassador that "all our arrangements are, it is understood, only valid if France agrees to them, for if she showed opposition nothing could be done."[9]

We shall now follow Thiers' critical reaction to the foreign policy of Napoleon III during the decade of the 1860s. His approval of the Crimean War and his dislike of the final outcome of that with Austria in Italian unity have been mentioned.[10] The latter especially was to him a source of concern for he saw in it a dangerous precedent for a similar, but far more significant, occurrence in the Germanic world, a prescient appraisal indeed.

### The Mexican Adventure

A dispute over the payment of debts that internal Mexican conditions made it difficult to discharge marked the beginning of the Mexican adventure. In addition to France, England and Spain had similar claims and the three countries joined in a show of force. This was in 1861. But while the last two named countries were content with the occupation of Tampico and Vera Cruz, where customs duties could be collected, France opted for deeper involvement in the troubled domestic politics of Mexico, allying herself with the conservative clerical party. In 1863 Mexico City was entered by French forces and a totally French-supported regime was set up in which the Austrian Archduke Maximilian, a brother of the Austrian emperor, was proclaimed Emperor of Mexico.

When Napoleon III defended his action in the speech opening in 1864 session of the *Corps Législatif*, the response was an amendment to the address critical of this and other distant entanglements. On January 26 Thiers delivered a very long speech on the subject, adding to his criticism the next day. He was not opposed to French imperial activity in general, but his view of the suitable sphere of that activity contrasted with the appropriately wider range of the British.[11] The proper range of the French should remain nearer home, the Mediterranean and Africa; of its extension into the Far East and the Pacific Thiers took a sceptical view. Mexico fell into the same category. Thiers insisted in particular on the risks that support of Maximilian entailed, and the problem in his estimation was how to extricate France from the compromising adventure with its additional risk of incurring American displeasure; the Monroe Doctrine was well known.[12]

Thiers' judgment was altogether sound and proved fully justified by the ultimate disastrous outcome. When gathering clouds in Europe caused the recall of the French force from Mexico, it was not long before France's adventure collapsed, luckless Maximilian being captured and executed by the Mexicans. The United States was indeed irritated, taking a stronger position in the matter after its Civil War was over. No better illustration could be cited of French meddling,[13] and one consequence was the lack of sympathy for France in the United States at the time of the war of 1870.

Speaking immediately after the news of Maximilian's execution was received, Thiers put the episode in a larger context, using it as an illustration of the fact that the cause of the misadventure was "the lack of control in the organization of our government,"[14] in other words the too great power of the executive.

## The Awkward Italian Situation

By 1867, when Maximilian met his fate, largely as a consequence of French abandonment, there were indeed dark clouds on the European horizon. From Italy to Prussia, by way of Austria and through the minor incidents that were the affair of the Danish Duchies and of Luxembourg, the direction of the course of events is steady and clear. The directing hand throughout the second half of the decade of the 1860s is that of the Prussian Minister President, Otto von Bismarck, one of the outstanding diplomats of all time, if not personally a very attractive character. Thiers understood the situation well as shown by his appraisals and warnings.

We must go back a little in time to pick up the thread of Italian affairs. The making of the Kingdom of Italy in 1861 left that creation incomplete, for it lacked the two important cities that were Venice and Rome; if the validity of the principle of nationality is granted, their eventual integration into the rest must be the two chief concerns of Italian foreign policy. Yet it was in some ways a paradoxical situation. For Venice was still Austrian so that the acquisition of it meant a continuation of the anti-Austrian thrust of the *Risorgimento*, but what kept Rome in papal possession was the presence of France, in large measure the maker of Italy.

An attempt to resolve the dilemma was the Franco-Italian Convention of September 1864. French forces would be withdrawn from Rome in exchange for an Italian commitment to respect the independence of that city. As a token of the earnest of that commitment the Italian capital would be moved from Turin to Florence, which it was in 1865. Needless to say, Napoleon III defended the arrangement in the opening session of the *Corps Législatif* at the end of 1864.

Speaking at length on the subject on April 13 and 15, Thiers poured scorn on the arrangement, asserting that Florence, whither the Italian capital had been transferred, was but a halting place on the way to Rome, which Italy had carefully not renounced, merely promising to refrain from direct aggression. He pointed out again that Italian unity was a mistake in view of the great diversity of the parts of the peninsula, but it was now too late for any other solution. He also considered at length the validity of the papal claim, pointing out that a state need not be committed to any particular form of religion but could accommodate all in equal freedom, citing the example of France, overwhelmingly Catholic but where Protestants and Jews could practice their respective religions unimpeded. The French defense of the Pope was outdated, and in any event it would be difficult for French forces to return to Rome should the turn of Italian events point to the need of such action.

For the rest, he set no store by Italian gratitude which would only last as long as Italian weakness. And he pointed out in addition that the anti-Austrian tradition in France was also outdated and that France should instead cultivate Austria. For he already sensed the Prussian threat under the leadership of an ambitious Bismarck and, as pointed out before, in Italian unity he saw a regrettable model and encouragement for a comparable German development.

### The French Defeat at Sadowa

His fears were to materialize perhaps even sooner than he expected. The same year 1864 saw the imbroglio of the Danish Duchies, an episode in the unfolding of which one can only use the homely expression that Bismarck led Austria by the nose. Exploiting with skill the complications that grew out of the issue of succession, the constitutional position of the Danish crown in the Duchies of Schleswig and Holstein, the former partly the other wholly German, Bismarck contrived to have Austria join Prussia in war against Denmark, a war presented as an enterprise in the defense of Germandom.

But this was only a step in a larger scheme. For the arrangement that he contrived with Austria, the Convention of Gastein, was merely a device intended for picking a quarrel with her, whom he challenged for leadership of the Germanic world. The skill of his maneuvering can only command respect, for Austria was a major European power not to be challenged lightly. So he contrived to enlist Russian sympathy and French neutrality as well as an alliance with Italy.

Thiers observed the trend of events with alarm. The speech he gave on May 3, 1865 is an impressive analysis and forecast. Bismarck, according to him, had acted with illegal high-handedness in the affair of the Duchies. The principle of nationality once again Thiers rejected, even indulging in a somewhat pathetic appeal to the Germanic peoples to preserve their distinct identities. But, more important, he saw in the continued fragmentation of the Germanic world one of the fundamental bases of the whole European equilibrium. As he put it on a later occasion, after the deed had been done, "the European equilibrium is not a situation, it is a principle";[15] small states were a necessity for the preservation of that equilibrium, and French liberalism had mistakenly let itself be led astray by its own inner tendencies. "The principles of domestic policy must never be those of foreign policy."[16] Thiers understood *Realpolitik,* that German word for what some have considered a French practice.

Going back to his speech of May 1865, *before* the Austro-Prussian War, his accurate forecast of the future must be quoted:

What is certain is that, if she [Prussia] is successful in the war, she will absorb some of the northern German states; the rest will have representation in a Diet under her influence.

She will therefore have a part of the German people under her direct authority, and exercise control over the rest, after which Austria will be admitted as a *protégé* in this new order of things.

And then, allow me to say it to you, will be accomplished a great transformation, toward the realization of which things have been moving for a century; we shall witness the making of a new Germanic empire which was once centered in Vienna, and which now would be focused in Berlin . . . and to complete the parallel, this empire of Charles V, instead of being attached to Spain, as in the fifteenth and sixteenth centuries, would be connected with Italy.

Allowing for the dramatic form of the prediction and that dynastic connections no longer carried the weight they had in the sixteenth

century, it may be pointed out that as recently as the 1930s German
policy was trying to contrive the encirclement of France along the
Rhine, the Alps, and the Pyrenees. To his gloomy appraisal Thiers
added a clear statement of his understanding of what the European
order should be:

> The European equilibrium consists in the constant care of all nations, in
> modern times, in watching one another . . . in preventing any one of them
> from assuming proportions disquieting to the independence of all, and in
> joining to resist it for the sake of the preservation of an equilibrium of the
> European forces.[17]

Events soon proved the adequacy of Bismarck's preparations,
both military and diplomatic. When the Prussian army met the
Austrian at Sadowa on July 3 the result was a decisive victory for the
former. The encounter was a close call, the Italian diversion of
Austrian forces possibly having made the difference. In any case the
war was over. The Italians themselves were defeated, but their
share in the Prussian victory was the acquisition of Venice, while the
Germanic world was reorganized very much along the lines of
Thiers' prediction.

These matters were discussed in the *Corps Législatif* the following March, on which occasion Thiers had much to say in regard to
the changed situation of Europe.[18] For the government's attempt to
put a good face on the outcome, the reorganization of the Germanic
world into three segments, the North German Confederation, the
South German, and the Austrian domain proper, an intra-German
equilibrium that could be a prelude to a larger European federation,
he had little but scorn. Berlin had displaced Vienna, Prussian and
Russian interests were in agreement, and international leadership
had passed from French to Prussian hands. He still favored an English alliance and thought that France should endeavor to assume
the leadership of all those interests that were threatened by the new
rising power; but he had to acknowledge that France was isolated.[19]
Sadowa was a French defeat quite as much as it was an Austrian.

### IV   *On the Road to Disaster*

The parliamentary session closed at the end of July. When it
reopened in November the Roman question reappeared. Garibaldi's
attempt on the city resulted in the reappearance of a French force in

Rome. Thiers had foreseen the awkwardness of precisely that possibility, but he felt that France was honor bound, yet his defense of the French action was also awkward.[20] Speaking again five days later, he heatedly responded to Ollivier's defense of the principle of nationality. In doing this, he was consistent but, as mentioned before, the position to which he adhered, while much could be said in its favor, was opposed to the historic trend, which undoubtedly was injurious to the international position of France.

The final and formal displacement of France by Germany took another three years. Where domestic affairs were concerned, there seemed to be grounds for hope of the realization of Thiers' desire for a modification of the regime in the direction of his preference; that is the reason why his criticism of the regime was cast in a moderate tone.[21] The elections of May 1869 returned thirty republicans, and by June the opposition was in the majority, Thiers being part of it. Napoleon III yielded to the pressure, instituting a more open regime in September, a reorientation confirmed by the appointment of the Ollivier ministry in December. Within less than a year, in May 1870, a wide endorsement in a plebiscite was the country's response. France seemed to be moving toward a truly representative system of government.

And indeed she might have reached that goal in peaceful evolution had not something else happened. The French emperor was an increasingly sick man, a condition that only served to accentuate the indecisiveness of his direction of affairs. We may omit the minor Luxembourg episode[22] and reach the final stage, for which, unexpectedly, Spain was to furnish the occasion.

Bismarck was following the French situation with attention. He had proper respect for French power and had no wish for a direct confrontation with it, but he seems to have come to the conclusion that France, passive so far, would not allow the final step of German unification. If conflict there must be, it must occur in the best (for Prussia) circumstances. Like that with Austria it must therefore be isolated while the military arm was made adequately strong.

Once more his calculations were implemented to perfection; Napoleon III was no match for Bismarck and in effect played into his hands. When revolution in Spain resulted in the search for a new candidate for the throne of that country, the possibility of a Hohenzollern prince was advanced. French objections to such a dynastic connection were generally considered legitimate by the other powers and the Hohenzollern candidacy was withdrawn. But the proposal was revived and this time accepted, in May 1870.

The French reaction was fairly unanimous and on June 30 legislation was introduced for an increase of the armed forces. In the ensuing debate Thiers defended the project on the grounds that the best guarantee of peace was a French position of strength, though one that would convey no aggressive intentions. His speech[23] was moderate in tone and he credited Bismarck with peaceful intentions as well, cautioning at the same time against falling into the Austrian error of unpreparedness in 1866.

A new abandonment of the Hohenzollern candidacy to the Spanish throne should have settled the matter. Bismarck was disappointed but France rescued him at this point. Instead of being content with what was after all a minor diplomatic success, she sought to push her advantage by extracting from the Prussian king, in his capacity of head of the Hohenzollern house, a further declaration that the question would not recur in future. Such a commitment King William would not make, a fact of which he informed Bismarck from Ems where he was vacationing, and where the French ambassador, Benedetti, kept insisting. This account, in somewhat edited form, the famous Ems despatch, was given by Bismarck to the press and had the intended effect of "a red flag on the Gallic bull."

From France came the initiative of severing relations on the plea of a Prussian insult. On July 15, 1870 legislation was introduced for war credits and a degree of mobilization; it was voted amid scenes of nationalistic enthusiasm. But Thiers rose to explain his abstention. He argued that war was not justified for a mere formality since the essence of the French demand had been acceded to. "Do you wish it to be said by all Europe that the essential had been granted and that for a mere matter of form you are determined to shed torrents of blood?"[24] Recalling the significance of the events of 1866 for France, he thought the occasion ill chosen to redress that setback, and to Ollivier's insistence that France could not accept humiliation, he countered that she was isolating herself. The session was tempestuous and he had difficulty at times in making himself heard. War was declared by France on July 19, 1870.

How accurate Thiers' forebodings were events would soon prove. There only remains to trace the sad and unrewarding role that was his during the conflict and in the settlement of it.

CHAPTER 13

# The Franco-Prussian War
# (to February 1871)

## I  The War

FRANCE entered the conflict in a confident mood; as in the first Napoleon's days, she would carry the war across the Rhine. But the current Napoleon was a different man from his uncle,—no military leader, driven reluctantly by circumstances, physically ailing to boot; and the country was unprepared for war, especially in comparison with Prussia.[1] The result of this situation was not long in becoming apparent: within six weeks of its outbreak the war was essentially lost by France though it took an additional five months for her to acknowledge the fact.

The course of the conflict itself and its domestic French repercussions can be briefly outlined as useful framework for the main focus of our story, Thiers' activity and role; these were of the greatest importance, especially in the aftermath.

Within two weeks of the outbreak of hostilities MacMahon was driven from Alsace and another large army under Bazaine shut itself up in Metz. Early September witnessed the disaster of Sedan, when a large French army with the emperor in its midst had to surrender. The capture of Napoleon III raised a new question which was promptly answered on September 4 after the news of Sedan had reached Paris. The Assembly, or a rump of it, proclaimed the fall of the Empire, adopting the motion proposed by Thiers to create a committee of government and national defense, Gambetta soon emerging in a position of leadership in the provisional government that shortly moved to Tours.[2] The *Corps Législatif* had in effect abdicated.

By the end of September the siege of Paris had begun. A meeting between Bismarck and Jules Favre having proved barren of results,

137

the war must continue, however hopeless its prospects. The French raised further levies, even surprised the Germans by the extent of their resistance, and Bismarck was annoyed at the futile stubbornness of their refusal to acknowledge their irretrievable defeat. At the end of October Bazaine with his army of 173,000 men also surrendered, an episode that was to lead to his subsequent trial and much controversy,[3] and which had repercussions in Paris. But the radical elements in that city failed at this time in their attempt to institute a prelude to the later Commune.

Besieged Paris did not lack defenders, though the military value of much of their numbers was questionable, and the Germans opted for reducing the city by starvation rather than attempt a military capture of it. Paris yielded at the end of January while a general armistice was simultaneously agreed upon. In effect the military war was over, but peace was not finally concluded until formalized with the signature of the Treaty of Frankfurt on May 10, 1871. The chief terms of the peace were the surrender by France of Alsace, save Belfort, and a part of Lorraine and the imposition of a five billion franc war indemnity.

During the last stages of the siege of Paris, on January 18, 1871, in the Great Hall of Mirrors of the palace of the French kings at Versailles, on motion of the King of Bavaria, the German Empire was proclaimed, the Prussian king, William I, becoming German Emperor. The ceremony and the locale were impressive and if the intention was to rub salt into French wounds a better way would have been difficult to contrive. The wisdom of the gesture is another matter, as the ceremony that took place in n the precise same surroundings on June 28, 1919 would seen to show.

Shortly after the armistice an election took place in France, on February 8, the outcome of which was the National Assembly that met in Bordeaux, whither the provisional government had moved from threatened Tours. As usual in such circumstances the Assembly was faced with three tasks: the liquidation of the war; the current administration of the country; more problematically, the drafting of new constitutional arrangements. In all of these Thiers played a leading role.

II   *Thiers' Activity during Hostilities, July 1870–February 1871*

Thiers' above-mentioned motion of September 4 was not followed by his assuming the leading role that might have been expected, not at least in domestic matters. He seems to have preferred to wait for the unfolding of developments before assuming such a role; for one thing he and Gambetta were totally at odds on the military possibilities, Gambetta still full of hopes while Thiers was convinced that the war was lost. But after the election of the Assembly and Gambetta's resignation at the beginning of February, Thiers emerged in nearly full control. His activity in the interval took a different form.

### Thiers' European Odyssey

France found no friends in her plight, to a point the result of the meddling foreign policy of the Second Empire, though Bismarck's diplomatic skill should not be underrated. But, especially as the fortunes of war went against her, the enlargement of the conflict or at least the interference of neutrals seemed to be her best card. It fell to Thiers to undertake the unrewarding role of seeking some assistance, a role for which his past record and his wide European acquaintanceship eminently qualified him, and a charge that he not too hopefully accepted.

He was in London from September 13 to 18. Received with deference, he spoke at length with both Gladstone and his foreign secretary, Granville, the latter more sympathetic than the prime minister. But the chief argument he used, the disturbance of the European equilibrium consequent upon a German victory, did not impress his British hosts; their immediate concern, Belgian neutrality, had been respected by both belligerents and in their eyes it was rather France that had posed threats to that equilibrium; a moderate setback for her was to them wholly acceptable. Landing back in Cherbourg and barely stopping in Tours, Thiers set out for Turin, where he was on the 21st. There were those in Italy, the king himself, not totally averse to aiding France—a Garibaldian legion actually fought in France—but two factors militated in favor of Italian neutrality. It was on September 20 that Rome, following the withdrawal of the French garrison, had been entered by Italian troops; also, France was being defeated. Through Venice Thiers reached Vienna on September 23, but from Beust, the Austrian chancellor, he obtained little more than expressions of sympathy. On through Warsaw he proceeded to St. Petersburg where he remained a week. Very well received and entertained though he was, he could not undo the results of Bismarck's Russian policy—and

Napoleon III's for that matter. Besides, Russia had other thoughts; two weeks after Thiers' departure, on October 20, Gortchakoff, taking advantage of the war situation, denounced the Black Sea demilitarization clauses of the 1856 Treaty of Paris.

Back through Vienna and Florence, Thiers was again in Tours totally empty-handed after his exhausting five weeks' tour of European capitals. As the course of the fortunes of war continued unaltered by patriotic Gambettan speeches, there was nothing for it but to acknowledge the fact of defeat, especially as the French populace was becoming weary of the hopeless struggle. Realistic man that he was, Thiers accepted this view and it fell to him and to Jules Favre to negotiate with Bismarck. The extent of Russian good offices was the Tsar's urging Bismarck to grant a safe conduct to the French plenipotentiaries. The account of Thiers' journey to German headquarters in Versailles is tinged with harrowing color.[4]

Bismarck was also anxious to put an end to the war. The value of the one card in Thiers' hands, a possible extension of it or neutral intromission, he did not underestimate: the Russian action held possibilities of British involvement,[5] in addition to which the British, and others, were developing sensitivity to the longer term consequences of too large German demands upon France. Also, Bismarck had to deal with his own military, a situation similar to that following Sadowa, so that, within the German context and in comparative terms, he represented moderation. His demands were severe enough, but the armistice and the surrender of Paris were arranged.[6]

*Thiers' Triple Function*

One issue that arose and that Bismarck exploited was that of who or what constituted the legitimate representation of France, the imperial regime or the provisional government. It was in fact in order to regularize this situation that the above-mentioned election took place in France on February 8. One of the first acts of the National Assembly, on the 17th, was, by a nearly unanimous vote, to elect Thiers to the position of "Chief of the executive power of the French Republic," recognizing thereby the unique place he occupied, an expression of which had been his election in twenty-six departments. He chose to represent a district of Paris. He would, according to the Assembly's mandate, "exercise his functions under the authority of the National Assembly, with the assistance of the ministers that he will have chosen and over whom he will preside."[7]

The word *Republic*, added at Thiers' insistence, gave rise to some discussion in a body of monarchist majority, but that majority was divided and was sastisfied with the explanation that the arrangement was temporary, pending future decision on the ultimate nature of the regime, a condition that Thiers himself emphasized in his acceptance speech on the 19th. As usual, the specific name of the regime mattered less to Thiers than the real structure and location of power.

Here was a suitable crowning of Thiers' political life. Forty years earlier he had been as much as anyone instrumental in causing the downfall of a regime. He bore no responsibility for the downfall of the Empire, but circumstances now placed him in the royal seat himself. Yet there was little cause for elation, for the burden that he was assuming was a heavy one indeed, his responsibility commensurate with his power, being at once, for the time being at least, chief executive and prime minister, as well as retaining his position of simple deputy. If there is no question that Thiers was an ambitious man and enjoyed the exercise of power, neither is his patriotism open to question.

The first task was the negotiation of peace. Leaving Bordeaux for Paris, he thence went on to meet Bismarck in Versailles on February 21st. Bismarck was friendly enough but little inclined to concessions; the most that Thiers could extract from him was the retention of Belfort[8] and a reduction of the indemnity from six to five billion francs. Bismarck was in a hurry.

Dashing back to Bordeaux Thiers presented the terms of peace to the Assembly where his heartrending task was that of defending them, even in the face of the moving plea of the representatives of Alsace who protested against their abandonment. His argument was as simple as it was unanswerable: there was no choice.[9] Ratification was approved by a vote of 543 to 107 on March 1.

But there was still much to do. Two urgent tasks faced the government: a prompt return of the Assembly to or near Paris, the better to deal with the situation in the capital, of which more presently; financial arrangements for the discharge of the war indemnity, the first installment of which was due almost immediately.

Once the Assembly had accepted the terms of peace, the final

reestablishment of it became a formality and the German withdrawal could commence. On March 10 a debate took place in the
Assembly on the subject of moving from Bordeaux. The Germans
had marched down the Champs Élysées in the midst of dead si-
lence, but had departed from the city after two days. Various alter-
natives were suggested for the seat of the government, Paris itself
being excluded because of its highly disturbed and uncertain condition, Bourges and Fontainebleau also, but Thiers had his way with
Versailles, where the Assembly was to gather again on March 20.

During the discussion the constitutional issue threatened to
reemerge. Thiers succeeded in shunting it aside on the plea that it
could wait on the more urgent task of reconstruction:

> In order to reorganize you need not do anthing that will divide you. . . .
> Let us acknowledge freely that you are divided between two great par-
> ties. The one, and it is entirely legitimate and respectable, believes that
> France can only find lasting quiet under a constitutional monarchy. . . .
> The other, with equal sincerity . . . believes that something draws the
> present generation toward the republican form. . . . A number of en-
> lightened and generous men hold this second view from the depth of their
> soul. . . .
> Too often, gentlemen, we accuse each other unjustly. . . . Let us respect
> each other's opinion.[10]

The divided Royalist majority and the hopeful republicans were
willing to postpone a decision on the constitutional question in what
is referred to as the Pact of Bordeaux.

### III   *The Parisian Commune*

Thiers' brief visit to Paris had convinced him that conditions in
the capital made it an undesirable locale for the seat of the government. He was qualified to know the influence of the Parisian mob on
earlier occasions, in the 1790s and in 1848. In fact the same
phenomenon recurred, which has come down in history under the
label of the Commune.

That episode, which lasted some two months, from March
through May, has given rise to much discussion, been the source of
an extensive literature, and far exceeded the confines of merely
French affairs; in one interpretation it has been presented as a
critical occurrence in the unfolding of the Marxist influence.[11]
There is no room to go into a full account of the Commune, Thiers'

role in it, which was a crucial one, remaining our concern. A bare outline of its high points will suffice.

Ther German siege had reduced the French capital to a parlous condition, economic activity largely brought to a standstill, which meant in turn unemployment and political unrest, not to mention a widespread sense of betrayal directed at the provisional goverment; an appreciable segment of the Parisian populace entertained the not very consistent emotions of anti-German and anti-French government feelings. Paris also contained a large radical element, republican in the context of the day, while the majority of the Assembly was of monarchist and conservative inclination, in which respect it and Thiers shared the same views on the score of mob rule. The French phenomenon was about to be repeated once more—a clash between the radical capital and the more conservative rest of the country.

The Assembly's decision to cancel the pay of the National Guard, in large measure a subsidy to the unemployed, to end the moratorium on debt and rent payments was the spark that set the tinder aflame; in addition, the National Guard, not too dependable an element in the government's view, was to be disbanded. The attempt to regain control of artillery in the hands of that body initiated the clash on March 18. By the 26th local elections resulted in the constitution of a government, the Commune, of markedly radical bent, which in addition had hopes of extending its sway to the entire country. As similar occurrences that took place in other cities, Lyons, Le Creusot, Toulouse, and some others, were quickly put down, the issue became sharply one of Paris versus France.

On that score, the centralized unity of the country, Thiers would not compromise. His decision, owing to inadequate and undependable force, was to abandon the city, then to reconquer it. It was the plan he had entertained in 1848 and for the carrying out of which in Vienna he admired Windischgrätz. A sufficiently large and dependable armed force must therefore first be organized, in part from returned prisoners of war that Bismarck was quite willing to see used for the purpose; civil war in France did not reduce his bargaining advantage.

The collection of this adequate and dependable force was the reason for delay. Leaving aside local events in the capital, it suffices to say that by the end of May Thiers was ready. Government troops entered the city on the 21st, following which there ensued the "bloody week" during which Paris was gradually reconquered. It was a bloody episode indeed, for feeling ran high on both sides, as is apt to be the case in civil war. Of the insurrectionists, or *fédérés*, twenty thousand were killed; on their side they executed some hostages and set the Tuileries on fire, as well as the Hôtel de Ville and other notable buildings. The *colonne* Vendôme had been pulled down and the Paris Commune decided that Thiers' own house should be razed and his possessions dispersed. The list of epithets accompanying Thiers' name in the local press of the period makes a long and colorful roster.[12]

But these were hardly the motivation for ferocious revenge on Thiers' part. In his eyes the threat to the social order and to the unity of the country were what really mattered; the vile multitude must be unmercifully crushed, 38,000 people were arrested; many of these were tried, some executed, and seven thousand deported. Thiers had once more saved the country in one version—for the bourgeois at least; his hands dripping with blood in another, he had without a doubt seriously set back the workers' movement. He had certainly contributed to the perpetuation of the social cleavage that has been characteristic of France since her Great Revolution and has not to this day been fully reconciled.

That the part played by Thiers in these events (the war in some degree, overwhelmingly in the making of the peace and the crushing of the Commune) is of the highest importance would be hard to gainsay. As early as May 22 he announced in the Assembly the imminent defeat of the insurrection. It was indicative of the prevailing mood in that body that it should unanimously vote a motion to the following effect: "The National Assembly declares that the armies of land and sea, that the Chief of the executive power of the French Republic, have deserved well of the country."[13]

CHAPTER 14

# *The Presidency, 1871–1873*

T HAT the crushing of the Paris Commune should have been
    Thiers' accomplishment more than that of any other individual
was entirely appropriate. For Thiers was the authentic embodiment
of the feeling prevalent in the country at large, overwhelmingly in
the Assembly. Republicans there were indeed in France, but those
who held extreme social views, the more radical *Communards*, did
not command a significant following save among certain sections of
the proletariat, the Parisian especially. France was still in her great
mass a country of peasants and artisans.

Thus a confusion arose. It is not unfair to equate, in the context of
their respective times, the 1871 *Communards* with the 1917 Russian
Bolsheviks, also definitely a minority in their country at the time. In
both cases the radical minority thoroughly frightened the bourgeois
establishment. Many among that class in 1871, and not in France
alone, reacted to the word *Republic* itself in the same hysterical
manner that their twentieth-century successors did to the Red
bogey, identifying reform in any degree with the destruction of the
social order. The background after all, especially in 1871 France,
was that of the first two Republics, the second one well within living
memory.

## I *The Task of Reconstruction*

To the consequences of this situation that was the constitutional
issue we shall presently return. But meanwhile France faced the
urgent need to reorganize its economic life and various aspects of its
administration, in the aftermath of an unsuccessful war.

The complete and easy success of German arms, if it registered
with accuracy a momentary relationship of power, did not mean the
destruction of France. Bismarck had had, and continued to have,
proper respect for French power, its military aspect not excluded.

145

Despite France's relative decline on the basis of numbers, industrial development, wealth, and economic development, all those factors that are the material components of power, the 1870 Franco-German confrontation was a fair match. Also, there was in 1871, in contrast with our more totalitarian time, no thought of keeping France disarmed. Prisoners of war were promptly returned, some to participate in the crushing of the Parisian Commune.

The task of reconstructing the shattered French military structure was promptly taken in hand. As early as the end of June an impressive military review of some 120,000 men was held at Longchamps, though it was largely a parade rather than a possible threat to the German force at the time. By May 1872 the bases of the new army had been laid. The German success naturally induced imitation. If the first French Revolution may be credited with introducing the concept of the nation in arms, the practice of conscription was rather a Prussian contribution. But to this Thiers was strongly opposed,[1] mainly on two grounds: one, the different social structures of the two countries; the other, his belief that numbers counted for less than quality and the training of a professional army. He insisted on a five-year term of service, the time necessary in his view for the proper making of a soldier. The final arrangement amounted to a compromise between his views and those of the Assembly.[2] In the process of reorganization the National Guard, an uncertain quantity, was abolished.

The war itself had been costly and there was also the large indemnity to be discharged. In brief summation it may be said that the finances of the country were handled with effectiveness, within an orthodox conservative approach. Clearly, the immediate demands could not be met out of ordinary taxation. In June 1871 a two-billion-franc loan was launched that was covered two and a half times. There was much wealth in France, and French credit, whether at home or abroad, could easily absorb the demands made upon it. Thiers himself contended that the burden, while heavy, could be carried without difficulty, a judgment that proved wholly justified. Also, in conformity with earlier precedent going back to the Great Revolution, provisions were made for compensation to those who had suffered losses from the fact of war and the aftermath of the Commune, the capture of Paris—Thiers stressing that, in doing this, account should be taken of the available resources and the poor should have priority in indemnification.[3]

The evacuation of the occupied territory was linked to the discharge of the war indemnity. As early as September it was possible to obtain an acceleration of the evacuation—six departments—in exchange for an anticipation of the payment of five hundred million francs and of certain facilities for the introduction into France of products from the annexed territories. Thiers defended the arrangement,[4] pointing to the small dimensions and to the temporariness of the economic cost.

By 1872 the financial condition of the country was on a clearly stable basis. A new loan was launched, for three billion francs this time, most of it intended for an anticipated payment of the remaining part of the German indemnity, not finally due until 1875. Despite a momentary hitch in the negotiations, hesitation on Bismarck's part in view of the domestic uncertainties of the French situation, on March 15, 1873, the last convention was signed and on September 6 the last German troops left French soil. The credit for this accomplishment, the source of unqualified rejoicing in France, in considerable measure goes again to Thiers; even if with ill grace, because of the intensifying conflict between itself and the President, the Assembly acknowledged again that he had served the country well.

The just-mentioned loan was oversubscribed thirteen times, a reassertion of the standing of French credit. This was the result of financial management, a subject that gave rise to much debate that there is no room to sketch in detail. Thiers had occasion to speak often and at length in these discussions[5] where two things mainly stand out. One was his adamant opposition to the introduction of an income tax, which he depicted as tantamount to double taxation. The English model he knew well, but in this case also insisted, basing his argument on a wealth of statistics, on the difference between the social and the economic structures of the two countries. The other was his persistent adherence to protection, a position he again defended with solid information, not all of it irrelevant or specious. Nevertheless, the fact remains that, modern man as he was in many respects, his image of France was not that of a country fully inserted in the trend of modern industrial development. On the whole he had his way, and the various commercial treaties that were a legacy of the economic policy of Napoleon III, the Cobden-Chevalier one of 1860 with England in particular, were gradually revised or abrogated.

Other subjects were also discussed, administrative reform and local government among them.[6] Thiers remained a believer in the desirability of high centralization, a conviction that the episode of the decentralizing Commune had only served to strengthen. Thus a long-standing French tradition was simply reaffirmed and in these domains little was accomplished. Lavisse's judgment is a good summation of the state of affairs:

> The French nation remained in the hands of a personnel of functionaries recruited from the bourgeoisie. . . . Save for a few *préfets* and *sous-préfets*, the body of personnel appointed under the monarchy retained its place, preserving, together with its esprit de corps, its contempt for those it administered, its suspicion of the elected representatives.
>
> It was a conservative reorganization, in accordance with the policy of the Assembly and the character of Thiers; it preserved the mechanism and the personnel of the monarchic regimes.[7]

This continuity in the structure of the French state, a source of strength in some respects, however also went with tendencies that may be described as sclerotic, at once cause and effect of a lack of adaptability that was to manifest itself in continued relative decline of position. But much of this has become clearer in retrospect, and to retain a proper sense of perspective there is no denying that the recovery of France in the immediate aftermath of the Franco-Prussian War was both swift and impressive, to the point that Bismarck wondered whether he had not been too gentle. To this outcome the "reign" of Thiers—he was often referred to as "the little king"—made a notable contribution.

## II   *The Constitutional Question*

The election of February 1871 had largely hinged on the issue of peace, for which the country was anxious despite some elements, best represented by Gambetta, who favored the hopeless pursuit of a war *à outrance*. So peace was the result, in the making of which Thiers' role has been explained, and he emerged in the position of well-nigh indispensable man, a fact that the Assembly could not help but acknowledge. That unicameral representation of the country was at the moment the repository of all power, and for the longer term the issue of the ultimate nature of the regime was paramount.

On the score of fundamentals, the structure of society, the Assembly and Thiers were essentially in agreement, believers both in a conservative orientation. Hence the irony of the fact that, for the two years during which Thiers held the combined posts of chief executive and prime minister, until his resignation in May 1873, relations between him and the Assembly became increasingly difficult.

### The Assembly versus Thiers

His formal title of "Chief of the executive power of the French Republic" concealed an ambiguity. Thiers repeatedly acknowledged that ultimate power resided in the Assembly at the service of which he remained, but this did not mean that he would not have preferred a more stable mandate, especially as he felt, not without considerable reason, that he himself was a more authentic expression of the temper of the French people than their elected representatives.

But it would be wholly erroneous to read into this judgment any tendency on his part toward a dictatorial solution; he steadfastly adhered to the view he had often expressed that Caesarism, entrusting to one man the destinies of the nation, was a risky arrangement. At most, by dangling the threat of resignation, he would coerce the Assembly into accepting his views—they agreed in their hearts that he was the indispensable man. That view was shared outside France. Bismarck, for example, was concerned in the last stages of the negotiations for the anticipated payment of the war indemnity lest he should have to deal with anyone but Thiers. The characterization of "the little king" had considerable justification.

There precisely lay the root of the conflict between himself and the Assembly. Thiers was a monarchist at heart, the July Monarchy ever his preference, and did not change his views on doctrinaire theoretical grounds. But he was also above all a practical man and there is little question that after 1871 he increasingly came to feel that the drift of French opinion was steadily toward a republican solution. What mattered a label after all? The real issue for him was that of structural arrangements, social, political, and economic, and the one important concern of legislators should be to insure that it would be a *conservative* Republic. As he put it, "the Republic will be conservative, or it will not be."

But, as pointed out before, the word *Republic* in the view of many carried connotations akin to those of the later Bolshevik menace. The Assembly elected in February 1871 was definitely monarchist in its majority.[8] But here another problem arose: who would be the candidate for the French throne? For the legacy of the 1830 revolution had been to produce two claimants for that position: the Count of Chambord, Henry V, the heir of the Bourbon line, and the Count of Paris, carrier of the Orleanist inheritance. Thus the majority was split, which was the reason for its acceptance of the *provisional* Republic, pending the day when it could resolve its dilemma.

It was a thankless undertaking which in the end proved insoluble. For the Count of Chambord was a true heir of Charles X, totally unaware of the conditions of the world of his day. The specific difficulty came to focus on his insistence on the white flag of the Bourbons. The issue may seem trivial, yet trivial it was not, for the white flag was intended, and taken, as concrete symbol of the denial of all that had happened since 1789. On such a platform the Legitimists were definitely a minority, and a dwindling one to boot; all other tendencies rallied to the tricolor. Thiers' quip was appropriate that the Count of Chambord deserved to be "called the French Washington, for he had founded the Republic." There was indeed republican rejoicing and corresponding consternation in the Royalist camp. The most that could be done was to allow the princes to return to France, where they were in fact elected to membership in the Assembly. Thiers accepted this, but only in exchange for their promise not to take their seats in the Assembly. But the monarchist majority in that body was irritated against Thiers, suspecting the duplicity of his maneuvers and resentful of his occasional tendency to adopt a lecturing tone. Skilled in the parliamentary game, Thiers kept in contact with both sides, though on balance his reassurances were found more convincing by the advocates of the Republic.

The Royalists had cause to feel concern though their embarrassment was mainly due at first to their inability to find a compromise between the rival claimants.[9] Thiers' observation was apt that one could not have three persons on the throne—the Bonapartist faction, momentarily discredited, was beginning to reassert itself. But in addition the Royalists misjudged the temper of the electorate; one evidence of this was soon forthcoming. On July 2 there were by-elections for the replacement of 118 vacancies, the result of multiple elections, Thiers' own for instance in twenty-six districts, as well as of some resignations. The result was a republican landslide, one hundred republicans being returned.

In view of the fact that the chief task of the Assembly—peace—had been accomplished, there was considerable feeling that new elections should be held for a body whose main function would be constitutional. But the Assembly persisted in remaining, its Royalist majority still hoping to resolve the dilemma of the two rival claimants. For that same reason it was also hesitant in dealing with the constitutional issue. Yet also desirous of curbing the executive power, at the end of August it enacted legislation that in effect was constitutional in nature though not formally labeled such. The so-called Rivet-Vitet law was in reality a dodge, or an evasion, for while asserting the constitutional prerogative of the Assembly, it stated that the title of the chief executive should henceforth be that of President of the French Republic, who, however, it went on to state, would continue "to exercise his functions *under the authority of the Assembly,* so long as it has not concluded its task, the functions which have been delegated to it." Thiers would in effect continue in his triple role; that presidential acts would need a ministerial countersignature, and that he could only be heard by the Assembly after having notified its president (speaker) of his intention to speak, amounted to insignificant changes. He would also have the right to name and dismiss ministers, an issue that would shortly recur.[10] In effect the Assembly decided to continue the provisional regime sketched in the Pact of Bordeaux.

A small step had been taken, yet not an altogether insignificant one. In the eyes of the country, and of the outside world as well, attention was focused on the fact of Thiers' new title. Bismarck for one was satisfied; in France he was a republican. And so did Thiers profess to be, in the first message he sent under the new dispensation,[11] asserting that he would continue to exercise his powers as he had been invested with them on February 17. He wasted little time before sending another message, on the 13th, urging the prorogation of the Assembly, which in fact took place from the 17th of September, to last until December 4. His hands would be free, though a committee of the Assembly was established to watch over his activity. When sittings were resumed he sent yet another message, an accounting of his stewardship, in modern American parlance a State of the Union type of communication, tracing the progress of recovery to that point.

### III   *The Final Break*

The year 1872 marked a lull or a pause in the conflict between the Assembly and Thiers during which a good deal was accomplished, as has been indicated: the army law, taxation, and commercial treaties were the substance of that activity. When the Assembly met again after its recess from August to November, another presidential message gave rise to heated debate,[12] for in it Thiers seemed to indicate a more pronounced republican inclination. As he put it,

The Republic exists, it is the legal government of the country: to wish otherwise would be a new revolution and the most dangerous of all. Let us not waste our time in proclaiming it [the Republic]; but let us use that time to give it the desirable and necessary shape. A commission named by you a few months ago gave it the name of conservative Republic. Let us seize upon that title and let us make sure that it is deserved. . . .

Any government must be conservative. . . . The Republic will either be conservative or will not be at all

a statement pleasing to the Right, but acceptable to a broader range of opinion. But the further declaration that

The Revolution of 1789 was made in order to do away with classes, in order that . . . the entire nation should live under the same law, bearing the same charges, enjoying the same advantages, and that every one should be rewarded or punished according to his deeds

earned the exclusive applause of the Left.

The Royalist majority was irritated, claiming that Thiers was breaching the Pact of Bordeaux, abandoning his promised neutrality on the nature of the regime. No doubt Thiers' choice of governing personnel was predominantly from the Left, a condition also resented by the Royalist majority.

Since the presidential message could not be debated, a commission of fifteen with a Royalist majority was appointed to draft a reply to the message, an arrangement reminiscent of the practice of reply to the speech from the throne. But Thiers' replies to the commission, when he was questioned by it, seemed uncompromising, and the commission in turn drew up a report suggesting the setting up of another committee to examine the question of ministerial responsibility, a tangential attack designed to curb the presidential power.[13]

Thiers' concession, the appointment of a Royalist to the ministry of the interior, did not suffice to satisfy his critics.

A diversion, or complication, intervened at this point, growing out of the agitation of which Gambetta was the main focus. This popular tribune, a convinced republican, quite capable of the resort to demagogic appeal, represented the more radical democratic tendency and was correspondingly, to the conservative view, the embodiment of anarchic disorder. Meetings reminiscent of the 1848 campaign of banquets were sometimes prevented through the use of the unrepealed state-of-siege legislation. But on September 2, under the guise of a private occasion, Gambetta in Grenoble delivered a speech that was widely publicized and created a countrywide sensation. Thiers was annoyed at Gambetta's unrestrained mode of expression and expressed his condemnation of it, but the government was attacked in the Assembly for allowing the speech. An agitated discussion ensued on the 18th, the government pleading inability to interfere with a private affair. The Duc de Broglie, returned from his English ambassadorial post to participate in the work of the Assembly, led the attack. Thiers felt himself unjustly criticized and replied with feeling and vigor. The outcome was a compromise on a motion acceptable to the government, which expressed "the confidence of the Assembly in the energy of the government and condemned the doctrines professed at the Grenoble banquet."[14]

It was but a passage at arms, and on the 29th the debate resumed where it had left off on the 13th. The commission appointed on that occasion, interpreting its mandate very broadly, asserted that the source of difficulty lay in the too frequent participation of the president in the proceedings of the Assembly and went on to advocate ministerial responsibility. Replying for the government, the Minister of Justice, Dufaure, proposed yet another commission of thirty to examine the problem of the distribution of powers. Following heated debate, in the course of which Thiers again defended his behavior, on the loyalty of which he insisted, the Dufaure proposal was accepted. But the vote in its favor, 372 to 335, was indicative of the growing weakness of the government and a presage of the impending break.

As pointed out before, there was no fundamental disagreement between bourgeois Thiers and the conservative majority. As he put it,

There are two countries [*patries*]: the first is the land. There is another, that of moral and public order, of the great social and political truths, which is no less important than the first.

And again on the same occasion:

It is not a question . . . of settling the definitive forms of the government; it is a question of improving on a fact that is certain, unquestionable, undeniable, for you would have to deny your own votes to deny it, it is a question of making the Republic conservative.[15]

Why then the clash? It was because the Royalist majority had correctly become convinced that Thiers had accepted the Republic whereas it still clung to the hope of a monarchist restoration; hence the sharp division between two irreconcilable points of view. Thiers wanted to put an end to the provisional state of affairs; he would acknowledge the constitutional powers of the Assembly, but Gambetta's advocacy of dissolution and fresh elections was not displeasing to him, correct as his estimate was that the trend of opinion was toward the Republic. The majority of the Assembly on its side, while insisting on its right of constitution making, wanted to exercise that right in the form of ordinary legislation, easy to undo—in other words, wished to perpetuate the provisional character of the system. That was the crux of the difference and the judgment has point that

M. Thiers' social doctrine separated him completely from the radicals: but he remains bound to them by this secret, innate, almost indefinable tendency which, in spite of the affinity of his interests with those of the aristocrats of the conservative parties, makes him, nevertheless, in his intimate being, a son of the Revolution.[16]

Thiers' eloquent, sensible, and on the whole conciliatory speech had not affected the determination of the opposition.

Another element entered the situation at this point, for it was the very time when negotiations were proceeding with Germany for the final liquidation of the war indemnity and for the consequent evacuation of France. The German ambassador in Paris, von Arnim, a rival of Bismarck in his own eyes and an open advocate of the monarchy in France, did not facilitate the task. He was eventually bypassed in favor of Manteuffel, the commander of the occupying force, who got on well with the French. Bismarck was following the

French situation with close attention; Thiers enjoyed his confidence and in France he preferred the Republic, thinking it a less effective government and an element of weakness. The overthrow of Thiers might cause him second thoughts, a fact of which the monarchists were informed by none other than the French ambassador in Berlin, Gontaut-Biron, a monarchist himself.

## Thiers' Resignation

But the signature of the final convention on March 15 removed the need for restraint on the score of the German negotiation. The recess of the Assembly from April 6 to May 19 was a pause, but the election of Barodet[17] in Paris appeared to confirm the danger of radicalism; also, the speech of Jules Simon, minister of education and a close friend of Thiers, at the Sorbonne, in which he asserted that the anticipated liberation of the country was the work of Thiers alone, further irritated the Right. The showdown was about to take place. Thiers' last-minute reshuffling of his ministry in a markedly Rightist orientation did not appease his enemies.

The Duc de Broglie, a man not devoid of political skill though a convinced Legitimist and a poor orator, especially in comparison with fluent and voluble Thiers, led the attack. On May 23 he presented an interpellation to which Thiers could not reply until the next day, in strict compliance with the recently established rule of procedure. His long and eloquent speech on the 24th, a by now familiar rehearsal, did not prevent the adoption, by a vote of 360 to 344, of what essentially amounted to a vote of no confidence in the government.

The Assembly met once more, for the third time that day, at 8 o'clock in the evening. It was to receive the letter in which Thiers offered his resignation, which was promptly accepted by a vote of 362 to 331. Crisis had been in the air for some time and the sitting deserves the characterization of historic occasion. Wasting not a moment, in accordance with a prearranged scenario, the Assembly proceeded to the election of a new president. Monarchist MacMahon, widely regarded as an innocuous political figure who could fill the role of chair warmer for the future king of France, by a vote of 391 to 196 became President of the French Republic.

The active political career of Thiers was closed. In his capacity of ordinary member of the Assembly he could still participate in its proceedings, but he only spoke in it one more time.[18]

# CHAPTER 15

# *Epilogue, 1873–1877*

T HE "little king" had been dethroned. Though the operation had been long in preparation and in the end carefully stage-managed, in Versailles, be it noted, rather than in Paris to which the government had not yet returned, there was concern among those who had carried it out under the guidance of de Broglie. Thiers was a fighting man and his popularity in the country was considerable, even in Paris which only two years earlier he had so harshly subdued. But Thiers, even if he entertained the hope of second thoughts in the Assembly (had not his proferred resignation been refused on an earlier occasion?) made no move and certainly did not entertain the possibility of a coup. He resumed his place as a simple representative in the Assembly, but did not actively participate in its debates, save on the one occasion when plans for the fortification of Paris, a subject in which he was well versed, were under consideration.[1]

Thus emerged the Republic without Republicans, as it might at the moment be characterized, under the guidance of an Assembly that would not dissolve itself, but insisted instead on its constitution making powers, yet at the same time persisted in prolonging the provisional situation in the hope of resolving the issue of rival candidates for the French throne. The new ministry, under the leadership of de Broglie, sought at first and with success to allay any alarm that its advent might cause either at home or abroad; Bismarck raised no difficulties in implementing the recent agreement for the anticipated payment of the war indemnity and the departure of the occupying force.

But the Royalist majority must despair. Elaborate negotiations went on between the Legitimist and Orleanist factions. Thought to have succeeded at one moment, they were torpedoed in October by the persistent intransigence of the Count of Chambord on the issue

156

of the white flag.[2] Still trying to gain time, the monarchist majority enacted in November the Law of the Septennate, setting the tenure of the presidency at seven years.

At this time also the trial of Bazaine for his surrender of Metz and his general conduct during the war took place. A military court found him guilty and sentenced him to death. The sentence was commuted to twenty years' imprisonment, but Bazaine unwisely managed to escape, thereby tending to confirm the widespread belief in his guilt.[3] The episode only warrants mention because of Thiers' staunch and persistent defense of Bazaine.

In May 1874 the de Broglie ministry was overthrown, Thiers joining in the vote of no confidence. The discussion of constitutional arrangements was droning on, when, in January 1875, in the matter of the mode of election of the president, one deputy proposed the substitution of the phrase "the President of the Republic" for "Marshal MacMahon" in the text suggested by the constitutional commission. The Wallon amendment was adopted by a vote of 353 to 352, and this is often taken as the formal date of the advent of the Third Republic in France. In a purely formal sense this is true, but after a hundred years have passed it is clear that the Franco Prussian War marked the end of monarchical rule in France, whether royal or imperial in name.[4]

Thiers' appraisal of the trend was correct when he had judged the republic inevitable. Yet the majority on the Wallon amendment could not have been slighter, and the Royalists, MacMahon included, did not yet lose heart. Having long overstayed its mandate, the 1871 Assembly finally disbanded at the end of 1875, elections for its successor to take place the following February. The outcome of the election was a clear republican victory in the lower house, but the previously elected Senate—in January—had a more conservative Royalist composition. A short-lived—nine months—ministry gave way to one headed by Jules Simon, a close friend and admirer of Thiers, a change considered a success of the Left.

The president and the majority of the Chamber did not see eye to eye and out of this condition arose an important constitutional issue, that of the powers of the executive, more specifically the right of dissolution of parliament. On May 16, 1877 MacMahon dismissed his prime minister, recalling in his place the dependably conservative de Broglie. This was the famous *seize mai*, an attempted coup d'état in a sense. The response of the Chamber when it reconvened after a month's recess was a clear vote of no confidence in the government, 363 to 158, whereupon MacMahon, the Senate consenting, dissolved the Chamber.

On the occasion of the opening of the debate in the Chamber, on June 16, a dramatic scene occurred. When de Fourtou, minister of the interior and long ago associated with Thiers, asserted that the credit for the liberation of the territory belonged to the Assembly, a republican deputy, rising and pointing to Thiers, exclaimed "*There is the liberator of the territory!*" The majority followed suit and, also rising, gave Thiers a standing ovation. It was sweet balm for him, and the scene has passed into French republican hagiography; but it also clearly bore witness to his definitely republican association as well as to the intensity of the division that rent the French body politic.

The government made use of the delay to which it was by law entitled and elections were set for October, during which interval it resorted to modes of pressure reminiscent of those of the authoritarian empire. But the group of 363 that had initially brought on the crisis remained a solid bloc; it rallied around Thiers who thus once more emerged in a position of leadership that, given the likely outcome of republican victory, could have made him MacMahon's successor in the presidency. The prospect was not displeasing to him, and he entered the fray as a candidate in his customary ninth *arrondissement*, preparing for the purpose a manifesto that has been described as his political testament.

The gist of it could be summed up in the phrase "*la République, c'est la necessité*" (the Republic is indispensable), though the document lacked the usual vigor and clarity of his declarations. Thiers was eighty years old. The stamina he had displayed during the war and in the period of his presidency, the three-year interval from 1870 to 1873, would have taxed a far younger man. He sometimes pleaded fatigue and asked forbearance when addressing the Assembly in one of his interminable speeches, and at one time may even have suffered a mild heart attack. But he had promptly and seemingly fully recovered, attending to his multifarious activities, the presidency, the management of the government in its various aspects, the raising of loans, negotiations with Germany. Ever an early riser, a brief siesta would suffice to put him in condition to attend to the social aspects of his position. His dinners and receptions were graced by the cream of society and politics, and in them he often held the center of attention, ever ready to discourse on a multitude of subjects that gave him an opportunity to display the wide range of his competence. His capacity for work was truly astounding.

His relinquishment of the presidency in May 1873 considerably eased his burdens, and he entertained the ambition of devoting time to his "beloved studies" and writing projects that he had once considered and for which he had even collected material, the history of Florence for example. In the autumn of 1874 he paid a last visit to Italy.

His Parisian residence had been destroyed during the days of the Commune and his possessions dispersed, though many of them proved recoverable. In part at least the state indemnified him for his loss and he took an intense and minute interest in supervising the construction of a new town house, to which he finally returned in May 1875. In the typical residence of a grand bourgeois he continued to hold brilliant court while tokens of gratefulness and admiration kept pouring in from many quarters.

Nearing the end of the eighth decade of his life, his energy was inevitably ebbing. Even his robust constitution began to show signs of wear and he had to husband his energy. His reaction to the *seize mai* was what could be expected; his active participation in the electoral campaign of the summer has been mentioned, and his willingness to be cast in the role of standard bearer of the republican tendency and possibly to succeed his successor in the presidency.

In the midst of this activity, on the morning of Setember 3, he suffered a heart or apoplectic attack. He was past medical care and the end came in the evening of that day. Active to the very last at center stage, he had been spared the humiliating disabilities of old age.

Thiers' passing was a major event, taken notice of in France and abroad in acknowledgment of his very long and large role on the French and the European stages. Even Bismarck, appreciably younger but nursing his rheumatism at Gastein, upon hearing the news at dinner, stood up and raised his glass to Thiers' memory. In France, the Chamber being in recess, MacMahon signed a decree ordering a national funeral. But the arrangement was changed to military honors only upon Madame Thiers' insisting on a pointedly republican manifestation.[5]

Thiers' disappearance from the scene had no effect on French politics, the current state of which could have been a source of satisfaction to him, to a degree a crowning of his work. The election was a republican success, a rebuke to MacMahon's attempt to assert executive power, and his place was soon taken by Jules Grévy. The bourgeois Republic of Thiers, the life-long monarchist who was capable of acknowledging, in some degree at least, the changing character of society, though still in infancy was being launched on a durable path.

# Notes and References

## Chapter One

1. He may best be described as an irresponsible adventurer though not devoid of a certain manipulatory skill. Thiers was his son by his mistress. His wife having conveniently died, he married his mistress one month after the birth of Adolphe, but shortly thereafter deserted her to pursue further adventures.

2. Eighteenth-century French moralist, author of *Maximes* highly praised by Voltaire.

3. Sainte-Beuve, Charles Augustin, *Portraits contemporains*, p. 438.

4. French marshal, who distinguished himself in the Napoleonic wars. As minister of war in 1817–1819 he was responsible for reorganizing the recruitment of the French army.

5. An hysterical episode of mob violence directed against ex-revolutionaries and adherents of the Napoleonic regime.

6. This and other quotations from the same work are taken from the fourth edition of Thiers' *Histoire de la Révolution française*, published in ten volumes in 1834. Vol. III, pp. 289–90. The translations are all by the author.

## Chapter Two

1. Sainte-Beuve, *Portraits contemporains*, pp. 444–45.

2. See below, *passim*. In particular at the time of his second prime ministership, in 1840, and during the second half of the sixties when he kept pointing out the danger of the foreign policy of Napoleon III.

3. The first two volumes were recast in 1828 and the original edition was soon followed by three others.

4. Thiers, *Histoire*, vol. V, p. 185.

5. Ibid., p. 219.

6. General of Swiss origin who served in the French army, but mainly known as a military critic and historian and one of the founders of modern military thinking.

7. Space does not allow extensive citations of criticism, but a useful summary may be found in Gooch, G. P., *History and Historians in the Nineteenth Century*, pp. 199–201.

8. Thiers, *Histoire*, vol. V, p. 412.

9. See for example Thiers, *Histoire*, vol. IV, pp. 290–92.

10. Quoted in Sainte-Beuve, *Portraits contemporains*, p. 474, from *Le National* of June 24, 1830.

11. Quoted in Malo, Henri, *Thiers, 1797–1877*, p. 82.

12. Ibid., p. 38.

13. A scheme that may be variously described as harebrained or visionary whereby the possessions of the Dutch king would be divided between France (Belgium), Prussia (Holland proper), and Britain (the colonies). The Dutch king would be set up in Constantinople while the domain of the Sultan would provide compensations for Austria and Russia.

14. Christophe, Robert, *Le Siècle de Monsieur Thiers*, p. 39.

### Chapter Three

1. There are many accounts of the 1830 revolution in France. In addition to the one in Ernest Lavisse's *Histoire de France contemporaine*, vol. IV, convenient and more up-to-date ones are those in Weill, Georges, *L'évil des nationalités it le mouvement libéral* and in Artz, Frederick B., *Reaction and Revolution*.

2. French publicist and staunch opponent of the July Monarchy as well as of the Restoration.

3. Cited in Malo, *Thiers*, p. 120.

4. These had to do with claims growing out of commercial activity and the collection of indebtedness arising from it.

5. Lavisse, *Histoire*, vol. IV, p. 371.

6. Ibid., p. 373.

7. Ibid., p. 373.

8. Ibid., p. 378.

9. Ibid., p. 380.

10. On Guizot, see below, pp. 75–76.

11. These are enumerated in Lavisse, *Histoire*, pp. 388–89.

### Chapter Four

1. See below, p. 72.

2. The Casimir Périer ministry lasted from March 1831 to May 1832. Feeling that he received inadequate support after a new election, Casimir Périer offered to resign but was persuaded to remain in office owing to the foreign situation, the problem of Belgium.

3. Speech in the Chamber on August 9, 1831.

4. Speech of March 9, 1832.

5. Speech of September 23, 1831.

6. Speech of January 5, 1833. For an account of Thiers' handling of the episode, see Christophe, Robert, *Le Siècle de Monsieur Thiers*, pp. 73–85.

7. Speech of February 15, 1833.

8. Senior, Nassau William, *Conversations with M. Thiers, M. Guizot, and Other Distinguished Persons, During the Second Empire*, vol. I, p. 42.

9. The powers defined the frontiers of Belgium, found for her a king in the person of Prince Leopold of Saxe-Cobourg, and eventually guaranteed her neutrality, but this was not accomplished until 1839, owing to the recalcitrance of the Dutch king.

10. The creation of Belgium resulted in the elimination of the fortresses along the former Franco-Dutch border, established as a guarantee against possible French aggression.

11. These quotations are all from Thiers' speech of March 6, 1832.

12. Speech of November 29, 1832.

13. Cf. Albrecht-Carrié, René, *Britain and France, Adaptations to a Changing Context of Power*, chap. vi.

14. This was the outcome of another conference that met in London in February 1830, when the powers agreed to the creation of an independent Greece, just as they did later in the same year in the case of Belgium.

### Chapter Five

1. Speech of January 16, 1833.

2. Speech of December 9, 1834.

3. Speech of January 4, 1834. The elections of the preceding June had returned critics of the government. The Chamber was adjourned till the end of December and the debate in question took place in January 1834. Thiers was minister of commerce and public works.

4. Speech of May 12, 1834.

5. See below, pp. 142–44. On the Lyon rising, see Bezucha, Robert J., *The Lyon Uprising of 1834*.

6. Speech of May 16, 1834.

7. Speech of April 6, 1835.

8. The information obtained by Thiers turned out to be incorrect, with the consequence that the plotters were not apprehended.

9. Speech of August 25, 1835.

10. Thiers, *Histoire*, vol. viii, pp. 505–6.

11. Speech of July 4, 1836, in the Chamber of Peers.

12. See below, p. 133.

13. Speech of June 15, 1836.

14. Speech of June 1, 1836.

15. There had been hesitation for some years after 1830 about how to deal with Algeria. It was about this time that the conquest began to be

extended, laying the bases for the nature of the French establishment, one consequence having been that present-day Algeria is in large measure, territorially, a French creation.

16. Speech of July 5, 1836 in the Chamber of Peers.

17. Speech of June 15, 1836.

18. As for example in his version of the French behavior in Algeria, as it appeared in an article in the *Morning Post* on June 30, 1841.

19. Lavisse, Ernest, *Histoire de France contemporaine*, vol. V, *La Monarchie de Juillet*, p. 128.

20. Ibid., p. 139; Christophe, *Le Siècle de Monsieur Thiers*, p. 131.

21. Christophe, p. 134. Thiers had been given the title of baron and made a commander of the Legion of Honor.

### Chapter Six

1. Speech of May 14, 1840.

2. Guizot, François, *Mémoires pour servir à l'histoire de mon temps*, vol. V, pp. 42–3.

3. See above chap. 5, n. 18.

4. See above, pp. 50–51.

5. Speech of January 13, 1840.

6. Speech of April 14, 1840.

7. Speech of November 25, 1840.

8. Guizot to de Broglie, the foreign minister, September 23, 1840. Guizot, *Mémoires*, vol. V, p. 371.

9. Speech of November 27, 1840.

10. See Christophe, *Le Siècle de Monsieur Thiers*, chap. vii.

11. One of the most distinguished lawyers of the day, active in politics and associated with the Legitimist cause.

### Chapter Seven

1. Speech of May 10, 1842.

2. Speech of January 20, 1842.

3. Speech of January 22, 1842; also of May 19, 1842.

4. Speech of January 22, 1844.

5. In Greece, too, British and French influences were in competition.

6. Rather petty—on both sides—squabbles centering around English missionary activity in Tahiti (the Pritchard affair) and France's handling of it. See Lavisse, *Histoire*, p. 309.

7. Speech of January 22, 1844, in the discussion of foreign policy in reply to the speech from the throne.

8. This speech is a particularly good summation of precisely what Thiers' position was and essentially remained.

9. Cited in Lavisse, *Histoire*, p. 315.

10. Like other aspects of French society, the organization of education,

especially since Napoleon's time, has been highly centralized, all aspects of it, from the lowest to the highest, being subject to uniform and country-wide regulation.

11. France had obtained the Pope's assent to the suppression of the Jesuits in the country. That congregation had, in liberal eyes, become the symbolic embodiment of all that was retrograde and opposed to the trend of modern progress.

### Chapter Eight

1. For Tocqueville's appraisal of the quality of political life in the country, see Lavisse, *Histoire*, pp. 320–21.

2. Speech of January 31, 1848.

3. See below, p. 133.

4. Speech of February 3, 1848.

5. Cited in Lavisse, *Histoire*, p. 380. This is a good statement of the precise meaning of Thiers' revolutionary sympathies.

6. Ibid., p. 382.

7. The preceding day, at Mâcon, a large gathering had held a banquet; the hero of the occasion had been Lamartine. His *Histoire des Girondins*, which had appeared between March and June 1847, had made him momentarily the standard bearer of the revolutionary ideal.

8. See below, pp. 182–83.

### Chapter Nine

1. Cited in Christophe, *Le Siècle de Monsieur Thiers*, pp. 205–6.

2. Though he himself, a Utopian socialist, was associated with the more extreme forms of radicalism. He was exiled after a brief participation in the government.

3. Of moderate republican inclination, Ollivier accepted office in the closing days of the Second Empire when the regime attempted a liberal orientation.

4. Session of July 26, 1848.

5. Thiers, Adolphe, *De la propriété*, pp. 14–15.

6. Ibid., p. 21.

7. Ibid., p. 48.

8. Ibid., p. 364.

9. Ibid., p. 412.

10. The problem of education was also discussed, but it will be convenient to deal with it later, in connection with other developments in that domain. See below, pp. 104–107.

11. Cited in Lavisse, *Histoire*, vol. VI, p. 125.

12. Ibid., p. 127.

13. See Christophe, pp. 207–14, for a colorful description of the dinner that Thiers gave to a small and select company, of which Louis Napoleon

was a member, on December 10, the occasion an enlightening commentary
on Thiers' mode of political operation.

### Chapter Ten

1. Speech of October 12, 1849.
2. One of the leaders and chief spokesmen of the Catholic party.
3. This and the preceding quotation are from the speech of January 18, 1850.
4. Bishop of Orléans, an exponent of the liberal tendency within the Catholic party.
5. Speech of February 13, 1850.
6. Speech of February 23, 1850.
7. Speech of January 26, 1850.
8. Thiers gave to Senior a very different version of the incident, claiming that the phrase was used deliberately for the purpose of rousing tempers and of securing legislation that would in effect substantially reduce the electorate, which purpose was successfully accomplished. Cf. Senior, *Conversations*, pp. 76–7.
9. Speech of January 17, 1851.

### Chapter Eleven

1. Senior's work is a highly useful source on French affairs, consisting of a detailed reporting of discussions with a number of individuals prominent in those affairs, as the title of the book indicates.
2. Senior, *Conversations*, pp. 118–19.
3. Malo, *Thiers*, p. 445.
4. Senior, p. 410.
5. Ibid.
6. The state of communications at the time—the telegraph did not reach Constantinople—of necessity gave greater freedom of action to the local representatives of the powers.
7. The international exposition of 1855 in Paris was calculated to the same effect of emphasizing the progressiveness and benefits of the imperial regime.
8. See above, p. 88.
9. Three main tendencies prevailed among those desirous of making a united Italy: a federation under papal leadership; a republican solution, of which Mazzini was the best known advocate; and union under the leadership of the Kingdom of Sardinia, the outcome that eventually prevailed.
10. The granting of a constitution, the *Statuto*, in the Kingdom of Sardinia in 1848 helped rally to Piedmontese leadership much liberal feeling.
11. See Gooch, G. P., *History and Historians in the Nineteenth Century*, pp. 201–5, for a good summation of the work and its contemporary reception.

12. This and the following quotations are all taken from the above-mentioned preface to the twelfth volume of the *History of the Consulate and the Empire*.

13. This is Thiers' concluding judgment on the whole Napoleonic episode and the moral he draws from the tale.

## Chapter Twelve

1. See below, pp. 128–29, 147.

2. An illegitimate half brother of Louis Napoleon, he had played a considerable role in the organization of the coup d'état and continued as an influential figure in the regime thereafter.

3. Speech of March 28, 1863.

4. Speech of February 26, 1866.

5. The Mexican adventure. See speech of July 9, 1867.

6. Speech of January 30, 1868.

7. Speeches of December 24, 1863, June 6, 1865, July 3 and 7, 1868.

8. See in particular his speech of February 23, 1869.

9. La Gorce, Pierre de, *Histoire du Second Empire*, vol. IV, p. 597.

10. See above, pp. 117–18.

11. See the quotation on p. 67.

12. British and French interest and activity in Texas, before its incorporation into the United States, had also been looked askance at by the latter.

13. Another illustration of it was the ineffectual French sympathy for the Polish rising of 1863, and the consequent irritation of the Tsar at what he considered uncalled for advice.

14. Speech of July 9, 1867.

15. Speech of March 14, 1867 in which Thiers gave a close and critical analysis of the record of French foreign policy.

16. Ibid.

17. The last two quotations are both from the speech of May 3, 1865.

18. The speech of March 14, 1867 marked a change in the direction of liberalizing the empire. Instead of the reply to the speech from the throne, the right of interpellation, of which Thiers availed himself, had been granted.

19. Speeches of March 14 and 18, 1867.

20. Speech of December 4, 1867.

21. For example, in his speech of April 2, 1869.

22. By way of obtaining some compensation in connection with the formation of the North German Confederation, Napoleon III toyed with the possibility of purchasing Luxembourg from the King of Holland. In this case also he met frustration, another failure of his *politique des pourboires*.

23. Speech of June 30, 1870.

24. Speech of July 15, 1870.

*Chapter Thirteen*

The notes kept by Thiers with a view to writing his memoirs give his own contemporary account of subjects treated in this and the following chapters. These deal with his European odyssey in search of assistance from the neutral powers after the outbreak of war and the initial French defeats, his negotiations with Bismarck for the conclusion of the armistice and the peace, and his tenure of the presidency.

1. This had been the main reason for Thiers' opposition to the war, in which respect his judgment proved far sounder than that of the government.

2. From besieged Paris Gambetta escaped by balloon to join the government in Tours.

3. The failure of Bazaine and MacMahon to coordinate their moves was blamed on the former and he was subsequently tried and found guilty.

4. For an account of Thiers' trip to Versailles and Paris and his dealings with Bismarck at this point, see Christophe, *Le Siècle de Monsieur Thiers*, pp. 331–37; also Dreyfus, Robert, *Monsieur Thiers contre l'empire, la guerre, la commune, 1869–1871*, pp. 192–220.

5. The Russian denunciation of the Black Sea demilitarization clause resulted in an international conference that met in London in January 1871, to examine the breach of the treaty of 1856. Bismarck was fearful lest the occasion be used to raise the issue of the European impact of the current Franco-Prussian War and impeded the French representative's voyage to London.

6. Lacking any intromission by the powers, Thiers' negotiating position was inevitably very weak and he was left with little choice but to accept the German demands.

7. The Assembly had designated a commission of fifteen members whose function it essentially was to supervise Thiers' activity.

8. Given the cruelly humorous choice between the retention of Belfort and a German march through Paris, he unhesitatingly opted for the first.

9. Speech of March 1, 1871. Another tumultuous session the same day resulted in the Assembly declaring, six votes short of unanimity, the downfall of Napoleon III and his dynasty.

10. Speech of March 1, 1871.

11. Marx's *The Civil War in France* has become a classic of socialist literature.

12. Dreyfus, *Monsieur Thiers*, pp. 334–35. The literature on the episode of the *Commune* is extensive. Among descriptive accounts may be cited Dreyfus, chap. vii, and Christophe, chap. xiv.

13. In the session of May 22, 1871, following Thiers' account of the operations for the recapture of Paris.

## Chapter Fourteen

1. Thiers asserted his position repeatedly. See in particular his speeches in the Assembly on June 8 and 10, 1872.

2. While the principle of universal obligation was accepted it was in practice modified by a variety of exemptions.

3. Speech of August 5, 1871.

4. Speech of September 16, 1871.

5. The major part of Thiers' speeches in the Assembly from January to July, 1872, dealt with financial and economic matters.

6. The question of education also came up and was occasion for the continuing debate centering around the role of the state, an issue characteristic of nineteenth-century French politics.

7. Lavisse, *Histoire*, vol. VII, p. 336.

8. The election of February 18, 1871 had focused on the war situation and the issue of peace. For that reason it was a distorted expression of the feeling of the country on the longer term problem of the ultimate nature of the regime.

9. The Royalist factions thought to have found a solution in rallying around the Count of Chambord who, having no issue, would then be succeeded by the Count of Paris. But that scheme foundered on the Count of Chambord's intransigence on the issue of the flag.

10. See below, p. 153 on the issue of ministerial responsibility.

11. On September 1, 1871.

12. Thiers' message of November 13, 1872 from which the following quotations are taken.

13. The position taken by Thiers at this time is of special interest when compared with his earlier stand on the issue of ministerial responsibility, when he himself had been in the opposition.

14. Session of November 18, 1872.

15. Thiers' message of March 4, 1873.

16. Dreyfus, Robert, *La République de Monsieur Thiers*, p. 279.

17. Barodet, radical mayor of Lyon, was presented as a candidate and won a by-election in Paris against the more moderate candidate of the government. That outcome tended to invalidate Thiers' confidence in the conservative Republic.

18. On March 27, 1874.

## Chapter Fifteen

1. See chap. xiv, n. 18.

2. He even sneaked into France in great secrecy, but MacMahon, although himself a Royalist, would not lend himself to the somewhat absurd plan of the Count of Chambord.

3. The verdict has been generally accepted by historians, but more recently a revisionist trend has appeared that places an equal share of blame on MacMahon for the bungling conduct of operations. See for example, Christophe, *Le Siècle de Monsieur Thiers*, pp. 391–93 and 410–13.

4. No formal constitution was drawn up for the Third Republic, the simple collection of legislative enactments bearing on the organization of the regime having the effective value of constitutional arrangements.

5. Christophe, p. 444.

# Selected Bibliography

PRIMARY SOURCES

These consist primarily of Thiers' own writings and speeches. The latter are to be found in the parliamentary records for the periods of the July Monarchy, the Second Republic, the Second Empire, and the National Assembly of 1871. *Le Moniteur Universel* covers the interval from 1830 to 1868, then the *Journal Officiel de l'Empire français* from January 1, 1869 to September 4, 1870, which thereafter continued as the *Journal Officiel*.

Thiers' parliamentary speeches have in addition been conveniently collected as *Discours parlementaires de M. Thiers*, edited by A. Calmon (16 vols., Paris: Calmann Lévy, 1879–1883). The last volume of this collection also contains Thiers' testimony before the commission charged with the *Enquête parlementaire sur les actes du gouvernement de la défense nationale* (Paris, 1871) and the one that conducted the *Enquête parlementaire sur l'insurrection du 18 mars 1871* (3 vols., Paris, 1872).

Thiers did not write his memoirs, as he had planned to do, but he kept notes with that intention. These have been published by his sister-in-law, Mlle. Dosne, as

Notes et souvenirs de M. Thiers. 2 vols. I, *1870–1873*. II, *1848*. Paris: Calmann Lévy, 1901, 1902.

Mlle. Dosne is also responsible for the publication of *Correspondance de M Thiers*. 2 vols. Paris: Calmann Lévy, 1900.

Thiers' book *De la propriété* (Paris: Paulin, 1848), and his contributions to the *Constitutionnel* and the *National* also belong in the category of primary sources.

Thiers' historical writings are:

Histoire de la Révolution Française, 10 vols. Paris: Lecointe, 1823–27. Numerous subsequent editions.

Histoire du Consulat et de l'Empire. 20 vols. Paris: Paulin, 1845–62.

A fuller description of the primary material and its location than space allows in the dimensions of the present treatment is to be found in the works cited below by John Allison (pp. 362–63) and the biography by Henri Malo (pp. 597–98).

SECONDARY SOURCES

These are abundant, and references to Thiers are to be found in the memoirs, correspondence and other writings of the large number of leading personalities with whom he was acquainted during his long career. For reasons of space, no attempt is made to list such sources, the following bibliography being confined to some general works on the period and to works in at least considerable measure concerned with Thiers himself. For the same reason, magazine and newspaper articles have also been omitted. A list of such may be found in the bibliographies of John Allison's work and in that of Robert Christophe, both mentioned below.

ALBRECHT-CARRIÉ, RENÉ. *Britain and France: Adaptations to a Changing Context of Power*. New York: Doubleday, 1970.
ALLISON, JOHN M.S. *Thiers and the French Monarchy*. London: Constable, 1926.
ARTZ, FREDERICK B. *Reaction and Revolution, 1814–1832*. New York: Harper & Row, 1950.
AUBERT, JEAN. *De Quoi vivait Thiers*. Paris: Deux Rives, 1952.
BELL, HERBERT C.F. *Lord Palmerston*. 2 vols. London: Longmans, Green, 1936.
BEZUCHA, ROBERT J. *The Lyon Uprising of 1834*. Cambridge, Mass.: Harvard University Press, 1974.
BINKLEY, ROBERT C. *Realism and Nationalism, 1852–1871*. New York: Harper & Row, 1935.
BOURGIN, GEORGES. *La Commune*. Paris: Presses universitaires de France, 1953.
*The Cambridge Modern History*. Vol. X, *The Restoration;* Vol. XI, *The Growth of Nationalities;* Vol. XII, *The Latest Age*. Cambridge: Cambridge University Press, 1934.
CHRISTOPHE, ROBERT. *Le Siècle de Monsieur Thiers*. Paris: Librairie académique Perrier, 1966.
DANSETTE, ADRIEN. *Deuxième République et Second Empire*. Paris: Fayard, 1942.
DESCHANEL, PAUL. *Gambetta*. London: W. Heinemann, 1920.
DREYFUS, ROBERT. *Monsieur Thiers contre l'Empire, la guerre, la Commune, 1869–1871*. Paris: Grasset, 1928.
———. *La République de Monsieur Thiers (1871–1873)*. Paris: Gallimard, 1930.
GOOCH, G. P. *History and Historians in the Nineteenth Century*. London: Longmans, Green, 1928.
GUIZOT, FRANÇOIS. *Mémoires pour servir à l'histoire de mon temps*. 8 vols. Paris: Michel Lévy, 1858–1867.
HAUSER, HENRI. *Du Libéralisme à l'impérialisme (1860–1878)*. Paris: Presses universitaires de France, 1939.

HOWARD, MICHAEL. *The Franco-Prussian War.* New York: Macmillan, 1961.

LA GORCE, PIERRE DE. *Histoire de Second Empire.* 7 vols. Paris: Plon Nourrit, 1896–1905.

LANGER, WILLIAM L. *Political and Social Upheaval, 1832–1852.* New York: Harper & Row, 1969.

LAVISSE, ERNEST. *Histoire de France contemporaine.* Vol. IV, *La Restoration (1815–1830);* Vol. V, *La Monarchie de Juillet (1830–1848);* Vol. VI, *La Révolution de Juillet et l'Empire (1848–1859);* Vol. VII, *Le Déclin de l'Empire et l'établissement de la 3e. République (1859–1875).* Paris: Hachette, 1921.

LUCAS-DUBRETON, J. *Aspects de Monsieur Thiers.* Paris: Fayard, 1948.

––––––. *Louis-Philippe.* Paris: Fayard, 1938.

MALO, HENRI. *Thiers, 1797–1877.* Paris: Payot, 1932.

–––––– ed. *Mémoires de Mme. Dosne, l'égérie de M. Thiers.* 2 vols. Paris: Plon, 1928.

*The New Cambridge Modern History.* Vol. IX, *War and Peace in an Age of Upheaval, 1793–1830;* Vol. X, *The Zenith of European Power, 1830–1870;* Vol. XI, *Material Progress and World-Wide Problems, 1870–1898.* Cambridge: Cambridge University Press, 1965, 1960, 1962.

OLLIVIER, ÉMILE. *L'Empire libéral.* 17 vols. Paris: Garnier, 1894–1914.

POMARET, CHARLES. *Un Vrai chef d'état. Monsieur Thiers.* Genève: Editions de la Frégate, 1944.

POUTHAS, CHARLES-H. *Démocraties et capitalisme (1848–1860).* Paris: Presses universitaires de France, 1948.

RECLUS, MAURICE. *Monsieur Thiers.* Paris: Plon, 1929.

ROUX, FRANÇOIS-CHARLES. *Thiers et Méhémet-Ali.* Paris: Plon, 1951.

ROUX, GEORGES. *Theirs.* Paris: Nouvelles éditions latines, 1948.

SAINTE-BEUVE, CHARLES AUGUSTIN. *Portraits contemporains.* Vol. II. Paris: Didier, 1846.

SENIOR, WILLIAM NASSAU. *Conversations with M. Thiers, M. Guizot, and Other Distinguished Persons, During the Second Empire.* 2 vols. London: Hurst and Blackett, 1878.

SIMON, JULES. *Le Gouvernement de M. Thiers.* 2 vols. Paris: Calmann Lévy, 1878.

––––––. *Thiers, Guizot, Rémusat.* Paris: Calmann Lévy, 1885.

SIMON, PIERRE F. *Adolphe Thiers chef du pouvoir exécutif et président de la République française.* Paris: Édouard Cornély, 1911.

SOREL, ALBERT. *Histoire diplomatique de la guerre franco-allemande.* 2 vols. Paris: Plon, 1875.

WEBSTER, CHARLES K. *The Foreign Policy of Palmerston, 1830–1851.* 2 vols. London: C. Bell, 1951.

WEILL, GEORGES. *L'Éveil des nationalités et le mouvement libéral (1815–1848).* Paris: Presses universitaires de France, 1930.

# Index

174